SIT DOWN AND SHUT UP

SIT DOWN AND

SHUT UP

How Discipline Can Set
Students Free

CINQUE HENDERSON

ST. MARTIN'S PRESS 🟥 NEW YORK

SIT DOWN AND SHUT UP. Copyright © 2018 by Cinque Henderson. All rights reserved. Printed in the United States of America. For information, address St. Martin's Press, 175 Fifth Avenue, New York, NY 10010.

www.stmartins.com

Design by Kelly S. Too

The Library of Congress Cataloging-in-Publication Data is available upon request.

ISBN 978-1-250-10188-4 (hardcover)
ISBN 978-1-250-10189-1 (ebook)

Our books may be purchased in bulk for promotional, educational, or business use. Please contact your local bookseller or the Macmillan Corporate and Premium Sales Department at 1-800-221-7945, extension 5442, or by email at MacmillanSpecialMarkets@macmillan.com.

First Edition: September 2018

10 9 8 7 6 5 4 3 2 1

To my parents—who set each of us free

CONTENTS

ACKNOWLEDGMENTS

Anyone writing a first book owes a lifetime of debts. My most permanent one is to my parents. My father, who as a very young man marched with Martin Luther King Jr., immersed us in books. My mother, who marched in life alongside my father, immersed us in love. We, their children, owe them everything.

My second debt is to my siblings, with whom I spent my early life roaming forests, climbing trees, and inventing lives for ourselves beyond the borders of the tiny world we inhabited so long ago. I feel proud of the adults you have become and precious about the past we share.

Ramesh Gajraj and Alejandro Ramirez, from our first days together in college, the enormous intellectual and moral demands we made on each other have lasted a lifetime. Without those demands and the friendship that accompanied them, this book would not have been possible.

No one championed this book with more enthusiasm than Ayanna Floyd David, a great boss, better friend, and artist extraordinaire. With her keen writer's wit she even christened it with its name. Her unwavering interest pushed me to expand the vision of the book from the start and, in the final days, encouraged me toward the finish line. I couldn't be more grateful.

Modupe Akinola, Liz Kirby, Natosha Reid Rice—the holy triumvirate of my Harvard days—have been loyal friends and confidants since we were undergrads together. They are and have been friends, wives, mothers, sisters, leaders of black men and women, and I consider it a blessing to be numbered among them. Modupe especially pointed a way forward for the book at a critical time, as she has at many points in my life. Each of them have my devotion.

Dan Sharfstein deserves a special mention. He read and improved my proposal for the book and blessed it to his agent, just as he read and improved my manuscript and blessed it as I sent it off to my editor. He and the brilliant Ann Mikkelsen buoyed my spirits at a crucial time, and for their years of friendship, I am thankful.

Kukhautusha Croom lent much-needed counsel and support, as she has for everyone lucky enough to call her a friend.

Anyone who has come within the orbit of Debbie Allen will understand my debt to her. No matter the many hats she wears— dancer, director, choreographer, mother—she is above all a teacher. It has been my great good fortune to have been one of her students.

Wendy Strothman took up my proposal with enthusiasm, helped hone it to a knife's edge, and sent it out into the world with her exacting imprimatur. Along with Lauren McLeod, she has guided me nimbly through every stage of this journey. For seeing the potential in me and in this book, I cannot thank her enough.

Steven Pinker generously offered his time, and with a single stray comment about the role of fathers sent me down a completely unforeseen path that led to one of the most lasting discoveries in the book.

Dolly Chugh and Rene Quon contributed much-needed advice at crucial moments.

Donna Cherry, along with Alan Bradshaw and Katherine

Haigler, maintained the integrity of the book throughout its many drafts.

Michael Flamini provided reassurance and continuity during the final stages of the book-making process.

If Helen Vendler, Seamus Heaney, and Henry Louis Gates Jr. helped form my adult mind, then the following incomparable list—Ms. James, Ms. Williams, Ms. Anderson, Ms. Chappel, Ms. Ellis, Ms. Leverette, Ms. Brown, Ms. Turner, Ms. Price, Ms. Broom, Ms. Earney, Ms. Gandersman, Ms. Hope, Ms. Moureaux, and Ms. Seavey—of my public school teachers formed my youthful one. I am the writer they made.

I cannot, of course, end this without thanking the marvelous Karen Wolny, marvelous editor and human being. A simple but incisive comment early on in the writing transformed the nature of this book and enriched it beyond measure. She held my hand through every stage of its creation and, in the most fundamental way, it would not exist without her. For that I am eternally grateful.

Introduction

I was staring at a football player. His shoulders were bent, but he was not crouched for a blitz. He was eyeing me straight on. Even without pads he was massive. The air in the room was fire-hot, muggy. Any sudden move and this whole place would explode. He and I were not friends.

He was coming for me pretty hard along with his lady friend, whom the whole class called Booty, despite my effort to explain that no young woman should allow people to delegitimize her by naming her after a body part, no matter its prominence. (Would Oprah allow someone to call her Booty? Would Michelle Obama? Would Lupita Nyong'o?) Booty was having none of it.

I was at Countee Cullen High School in the heart of South Watts. Not long before, a freshman had been shot outside the school. Its history of racial and student violence goes back decades, but I didn't know any of that at the time. All I knew was that two dozen high school students were watching and waiting to see what I would do. And I was watching too, because the football player was cursing me in the worst way. Maybe I'd told him to sit down one too many times. Or to stop distracting the class while I'm teaching. Whatever it was, I had set him off.

"Motherfucker, fuck you. You don't run shit up in here. What you gon' do?" Yeah, he was cursing me out pretty bad and baiting me for a fight. And frankly he had a good question: What *was* I gonna do? I hadn't figured that out yet. Because in the back of my mind, I was thinking about those YouTube videos of kids fighting teachers and how at least half the time the teacher gets rocked. Hard. And I had bones, an ego, and expensive glasses and didn't need any of those crushed. I shrugged and forced myself to sound cool, even casual: "Probably call the guard."

It was so offhand, you'd have thought we were discussing the color blue. I was nervous and struggling not to show it. The kids were still watching to see who was going to win. It was in my best interest that I did. Someone shifted in their seat.

The kid doubled down. "I don't give a fuck! Call the guard! Urkel-looking motherfucka."

Laughter and commentary from the kids: "He called that fool 'Urkel.'" This wasn't going well, but I sensed an opening.

"Did you just talk bad about Urkel?" I offered before I knew exactly where I was going. He was a little thrown. Something in my brain told me to pursue this line of questioning.

"What?!"

"Did you just talk bad about my boy Urkel?"

"I'm talking about you, fool. With yo bitch ass." Truth is, the name calling was making me see red. So I stuck with the 1990s sitcom theme to keep from busting a blood vessel.

"Well, you're out of line there," I told him. "No one talks about me or the homie Urkel like that! So I think it's best you go to the office and think hard about what you've done!" A few laughs and some quizzical looks from the rest of the class. I headed for the door while calling for the campus aide and keeping myself well outside the kid's body space. He just kept cursing: "Stupid motherfucka."

The aide arrived and waved the kid out, but the kid was working on a stem-winder of final curses. Maybe it was my pride, maybe something else, but I didn't want to let the recriminations go completely unanswered. My go-to is to say something funny, but the stress of the situation had thrown off my comic sensibility. "Okay, Santa," I said, switching fictional characters. "Merry Christmas to you too. Come back next year." The aide chuckled and I got a few more laughs from the kids. He took the student, who kept jawing the whole time. I went back into the classroom. The students were staring at me, some glaring, one or two smiling; others didn't know what to make of me. I pulled up my pants briefly so they could see my socks, and I made a show of adjusting my glasses, the way Urkel himself would do it. I turned directly to Booty with a less-than-friendly smile: "Now what are you saying?" I was hoping the mixture of nerdy weirdness and just-kicked-out-the-biggest-kid-in-class toughness would be enough to get her to give in, but she was staring daggers. I kept staring back at her, a direct challenge, the final risky skirmish in a battle of wills. A few seconds later she looked away, mumbling what I was sure was *not* the Lord's Prayer under her breath. A tiny win. Very tiny. But I took it. I looked up and out at the rest of the class. Someone said, "This fool crazy," as I stood with my socks peeking through the bottom of my pants. It was almost a compliment. Better to be thought crazy than a bitch-ass!

Air slowly seeped back into the room. I could feel the balance of power tipping back my way, if only slightly, but only God knew how long it would last. Despite whatever laughter I had generated in this contest, none of it felt very fun at the time. I was feeling nothing but nerves, trying my best to hold it together. I took a breath and launched back into the lesson, hoping they couldn't hear my heart pounding in my ears. "Alright, then, what were we saying about the hypotenuse?"

Yeah, I had the worst job in the United States. I was a substitute teacher in one of the nation's toughest schools and this was my first day.

Sit Down and Shut Up is an insider's account of life inside the forgotten precincts of U.S. public schools, and it's dedicated to one not-so-funny idea—the sometimes hysterical but often harrowing truth about that world: new teachers flee in droves every year from our toughest schools, and many veterans have left long ago because of the one thing they did not see coming: kids' chaotic, unchecked behavior that the adults and even the kids themselves seem almost helpless to control. And this insider account comes from one of the most unlikely sources: a substitute teacher. I know what you're thinking. *A sub? What the hell do you know about teaching in tough schools? All you did was babysit for a day or two!* Turns out, you can learn quite a lot from subbing if you pay attention. You're also thinking: *Getting roughed up by kids is the definition of being a sub. Being cursed out doesn't mean squat.* Yes, except I worked at one school where students assaulted three full-time teachers and one administrator. My experience was not unique. And what a lowly sub may lack in depth he can gain in breadth, by going, as I did, as a stranger into countless strange lands with an open heart and a questioning mind. I was curious, obsessed even, as I traveled from one end of Los Angeles to the other, from Beverly Hills to Compton and every neighborhood in between, to find the answer to an intractable problem: how to make public schools work for the poorest and most discarded among us. A man named Sam Choudhary, whom *Forbes* named a leader in education in 2013, said what every teacher in tough schools secretly knows and is embarrassed to confess: "Student behavior is one of the biggest problems teachers face."[1] In poor and underserved communities, white and black, I think it may be *the* biggest.

If you are black or a progressive liberal, I have just raised your hackles. You are on guard because you're sure you are about to read yet another narrow-minded, self-hating black conservative's wailing about the moral failures of black people or the poor. If you are white and conservative, you are quite possibly feeling giddy, because you think you are about to read a brave black conservative's trumpeting of the truth about the moral failures of black and poor people. Both camps are wrong. I've voted only for Democrats. I believe in the social safety net. I listen to NPR on my way to work. I believe global warming is real. And in the following pages I talk enough about the evils of racism, the horrors of police brutality, the failures of capitalism, and, yes, private and public character and ethics to both satisfy and irritate the hard-core left and right among us.

But one thing is inescapably clear. Education experts, parents, and politicians have for too long danced around what is happening in the most troubled schools, insisting on all kinds of random fixes for why kids aren't learning. A thousand different theories, a thousand different reforms: better teachers, younger teachers, school vouchers, school uniforms, smaller classes, wired classes, charter schools, partner schools, block schedules, mixed schedules, later school days, longer school years, arts classes, yoga classes, teaching to the test, abolishing the test, eradicating tenure, delaying tenure, more math, less gym, more instructional minutes, more planning minutes, more direct instruction, more group instruction, student-centered classrooms, student-led classrooms, higher curriculum standards, revising curriculum standards, kinetic learning, visual learning, teaching like your hair is on fire, teaching like you're about to get fired (because you probably are), smart chairs, smart boards, chairs that wiggle, desks that wiggle, classrooms with no desks, classrooms with no teachers—the list is truly endless.

But nothing has worked. Why? My central, bracing premise— that in our toughest schools it's not the teachers' fault, it's the students'—points to a larger social reality far more complex than anything an iPad or a yoga class can fix. But perhaps more important is that children are what a society makes them. So what did we as a society make? What did we, the adults, do that it got this bad? And, even more important, is it possible to make it better? I believe it is.

During my year of subbing in some of the most difficult (and some of the best) schools in Los Angeles, I realized that none of the answers to why inner-city schools have gotten so bad are obvious. Tracing the answers to their source meant tracing them to many sources. It meant seeing all the difficult aspects of black American life—persistent racism, poverty, police brutality, the legacy of slavery, and fatherlessness—in both old and new ways and finding the right language to think about them and through them. It meant investigating first principles. Why should we even care if students in the poorest parts of the inner city learn to sit down and shut up? Again, I thought I knew the answer. That year showed me I didn't.

In the year I traversed the breadth of Los Angeles County from as far north as Pacoima in the San Fernando Valley to north of Compton in South LA, an area of about forty-seven hundred square miles, I saw the inside of more than fifty schools and taught more than ten thousand different students—at elementary, middle, and high schools. Struggling public schools, thriving public schools; struggling charter schools, thriving charter schools; private schools where the kids were less than awesome, private schools where the kids were flourishing; parochial schools, Catholic and Episcopal; Jewish schools, Orthodox, conservative, and reform. *Sit Down and Shut Up* is the record of what I saw.

My life until then had consisted of some relative success as a writer, but I did not take a job as a substitute with any idea of generating a book. No. At first I did it as a lark. I'm a night owl and write deep into the early morning hours. If it were up to me, I'd be in bed at 4:00 a.m. and up at noon. Being forced to get up early twice a week organized me and made me feel a little less like a bum. But also my conscience was nagging me. I come from a family of educators. My father taught at a historically black college for most of my childhood, and when he died, several carloads of his students carpooled from across the country to attend his funeral. They just had to be there, one of them told me.

The most dramatic memory I have of my mother is of her sitting on the floor of our small home in the rural South, rocking back and forth, crying terrible tears, and just saying, "Thank you, God. Thank you, God," over and over and over. I was seven. Although her words were happy, she seemed to be in such pain that I asked my father what was wrong. These were tears of anguished joy, I learned. She had passed her teaching exam and was now qualified to be a public school teacher. I've never forgotten that. My reverence for teachers and education is a permanent part of who I am.

While my conscience was badgering me, I was wondering what was going on in public schools—I kept hearing the rumor of a new generation of terrible teachers who were apparently openly failing struggling kids. I had attended predominantly black, rural public schools only a generation ago in a state that regularly competes for last place in education, yet my teachers taught me and my siblings well enough that I was accepted by, and graduated from, one of the best colleges in the country. In fact, in the few years between my graduation and my siblings' graduations, my high school sent students to Duke, Harvard, the University of North Carolina, Emory, the Air Force Academy, and a slew of the best schools across the Southeast. Other students joined the army, some went into the NBA and into Major League Baseball, and a small fraction ended up in jail. I am, in other words, what my parents *and* my teachers made me. So who made up this new crop of teachers rumored to be such open and bumbling failures? I quickly learned it was exactly that: a rumor. And it wasn't a new crop of teachers. It was a new crop of kids. Hurt, resentful children of broken homes (or parentless children), learning in a society that was not ready or prepared to address the internal struggles that these kids did not create but brought with them nonetheless.

Some of the poor charter schools and traditional public schools I subbed in, full of black and Latino students, were spectacular places where students were taking a deep dive into learning. Some of the wealthy private schools seemed like educational hoaxes, not worth the tens of thousands of dollars they cost. But when a school was truly failing, it was because a kid could say "Fuck you, motherfucker" to an adult, be sent to the office, and turn up in my class five minutes later with a note from the office that said *"OK to return to class."*

Once upon a time philosophers, from Jean-Jacques Rousseau to John Locke, wrote long treatises on education alongside their masterpieces on political economies and the nature of man. Plato's *Republic*, in which Socrates asks how one teaches youth to love justice, is essentially a teachers' manual. But the great intellectual minds of our democracy are preoccupied with what they imagine to be greater concerns. In journalism ambitious reporters see the education beat as at best a way station, at worst a type of exile. As one national reporter told me, "Even among local coverage, education is at the bottom of the pile in prestige." I once took a peek at the home page of one well-known journal to get a sense of how little regard we have for public education. A quick sense of journalistic hierarchy, from top to bottom, ran thusly: world news, business, opinion pages, U.S. news, technology, arts, politics, fashion/style, movies, local coverage, sports, theater, science, obituaries, television, health, travel, books, and then, finally, tucked somewhere between food and automobiles, well below the virtual fold, was education. The education beat will rarely win you any awards, and, in some papers, even a death notice gets more attention than our nation's public schools.

I refer to Rousseau and Locke because what this year showed me, above all, was something that the philosophers may have always known: that the four walls of a nation's classroom are hothouse laboratories—chaotic, teeming, vibrant, tough—containing that nation's most vexing social issues. In this case, beneath the sound and fury of outrageous adolescent behavior lie titanic forces: the legacy of race and inequality, the price of generational trauma, the failures (and promises) of capitalism, the nature and structure of human consciousness. And that combustible legacy made itself plain in every single interaction I had with an unruly student, a desperate parent, an exhausted teacher, or an overworked administrator.

Though this book focuses on black and Latino students in the inner city, by far the harshest comment I came across about student behavior while writing this book was said of poor white students by a white teacher in the all-white, opioid-riven Appalachian region. In J. D. Vance's bestselling *Hillbilly Elegy*, a harried teacher remarks, "They want us to be shepherds to these kids. But no one wants to talk about the fact that many of them are raised by wolves."[2] The economic collapse that fosters adolescent chaos stretches across the country, no matter the race. Facing up to that, offering solutions (and explanations), is part of the very real business of this book.

The most clarifying and confounding comment I heard in this year of being a teacher-for-hire came from a teacher in his early forties who'd attended Cullen High School as a student. After a particularly brutal day, he remarked with confusion and anguish, "This school was always tough, but kids used to fight each other. Now they fight the teacher too." That phrase haunted me and it concentrated my mind. It was the beginning of a mystery. I realized he was right. There were plenty of fights at the schools I had attended as a kid. On the bus, after school, at school. An older kid who lived down the road from us once took a gun to school because he was being bullied so badly. But no one fought a teacher.

During this year I slowly began to understand that that seemingly simple shift—from fighting each other to fighting the teacher—was a sign that something unaccounted for had entered this world and destabilized it; a Rubicon had been crossed and a thousand tributaries flowed from it. *Sit Down and Shut Up* is about my journey to find the source of that Rubicon and its tributaries and to ask if the flow of that terrible river, as it coursed through the lives of the neediest black and brown kids across Los Angeles, could be stanched. Some of the things I found at the mouth of the river thrilled and surprised me, others shocked and saddened me. I imagine they will shock, thrill, sadden, and surprise you too.

Though the experience of black boys in white schools, which has been recently treated in the press, gets some attention here, this book is primarily about the lives of poor kids in our toughest schools.[3] These kids rarely grow up to experience the more "sedate" forms of racism—passed over for lucrative jobs and promotions, tokenized as the only black, profiled in stores they have the money to shop in—their lives and schools are too chaotic for them to advance that far in life. This book is about how to improve poor schools so those kids can have a chance to struggle for a better livelihood, not just struggle for their lives.

It's about what I knew, what I thought I knew, and most of all what I learned during my yearlong journey inside some of LA's toughest schools. It is also about the enormous number of teachers and students who rush into battle each day armed with hope and grit and who—despite the many challenges our schools face—try to carve out a place where students can learn. It is about the thousands of tiny gestures teachers make every day, gestures that involve compassion *and* discipline, sweetness *and* stringency, second chances *and* bright yellow lines in their effort to return a sense of normality to their environment, so that teachers can nurture, protect, love, discipline, and *teach* their students. Drawing forth, to paraphrase the poet, lilacs from fallowed land.

Kids' Rights, or by All Means Vote for That Idiot!

It was 7:00 a.m. and I was on my way to work. This time I was heading to City High, a traditional public school in midcity LA. My radio was tuned to NPR and someone was yelling about "kids' rights." The yeller was running for school board. I turned it off. I'd be yelled at soon enough. Truth was, I was still reeling. Not just because that kid at Countee Cullen High School had threatened me a few days earlier but because they sent him back to my class five minutes later with a note saying "*OK to return to class.*" I complained to the office after school, but I may as well have been speaking Greek. I followed Wilton Boulevard South from Hollywood to Koreatown and turned right to head toward the Mid-Wilshire neighborhood, a stone's throw from La Brea Avenue. I pulled up at the school on time. City High is mixed—white, black, Latino, Jewish, Armenian—and one of the oldest high schools in Southern California, one of those schools to which ambitious kids from tough neighborhoods are bused or that bright local kids attend because their parents can't afford private school.

As I walked the halls, I heard what felt like a hum—the normal sounds of teenage chaos but something else too—both similar to, and quite different from, Countee Cullen—though I couldn't yet recognize it. For a sub, every day is the first day of school. You're the new kid and you've got no friends. Every student is a potential ally or a potential adversary you've got to defuse. And you've got to size them up quickly. I had been told to (1) scout my building for the nearest guard; (2) ask if the phone in the room was working; and (3) if students say yes, I was to assume they were wrong and ask for the office number anyway. I'd need to call if the shit hit the fan.

Most resident teachers and administrators view subs sympathetically and are eager to help you out because you're a guest in their house. Others are more suspicious. One teacher used to push her desk up against the wall and remove her chair when she had to book a sub.* She regarded subs as lazy, and she never wanted them to have even a place to sit down.

But that day I was lucky. The teacher next to me was Leah Ibrahim. She introduced herself right away, then broke off to yell at a kid for throwing his football in the hall, and he had nothing to say. "We had a rough day yesterday," she told me. "A big fight on campus. The Latino and Armenian kids got into it. First one in a long time." Then, as the bell rang for class, she added: "If you need to send a student to me, feel free. They're terrified of me." With that assurance I closed my door and started my class. My day passed largely without incident.

After school I walked with Ibrahim to the faculty meeting (yeah, they make subs go to those). I told her about my experience at Countee Cullen. She said she was not surprised but that Cullen hadn't always been like that. "It used to be a great school." At the meeting she ignored everything that was being said and graded

---

* Though it can vary from one school district to the next, many teachers use automated systems to book substitutes themselves on days they will be absent. The largest school district in LA uses such an automated system.

papers until the union rep got up to talk about the upcoming school board election. She looked up sharply at the mention of one candidate. "That's the one who keeps talking about kids' rights?!" Everyone turned her way. (It wasn't only the kids who were terrified of her.) "If we want what happened yesterday to keep happening, then by all means vote for that idiot." Scattered laughter, nods of agreement. "These kids have a right to shut up and sit down," she mumbled in a stage whisper and went back to grading.

In fact, she loved this school. She had left for a few years to teach at a prestigious public school nearby, but she didn't like it. "I like regular kids, Henderson. And the ones we have here are every bit as bright as they were." I agreed with her. Even though I'd been at this for just a few days at that point, I'd already met a genius or two. One kid at Cullen laughed at me when I tried to do a massive cross-multiplication problem on the board, carrying the one and all that. He looked at it and in three seconds spat out the right answer. I was in awe.

But, like a lot of veterans, Ibrahim no longer was so hopeful. "This is the worst time ever to be a teacher, son. These kids—" she said, breaking off her thought. "It was never this rough before." As the faculty meeting at City High let out, I saw her picture on the wall of the library. She had been voted teacher of the year by students a few times. We walked out of the meeting together. She was still grousing. She told me how much rougher the school had gotten lately, the increasing frequency of fights between the Armenian kids and the Mexican kids. One kid, she said, was a constant bully. After his umpteenth fight the school managed to get him kicked out, and he transferred to a charter school. But he returned with a lawyer who claimed the boy was being denied his right to an education because the charter school was not within walking distance of his home. "This kid fought every day. He even went after the assistant principal once. And *we're* denying *him* an education?" She asked if I would be going back to Countee Cullen. I said that, despite the craziness, I kind of liked it. She asked for my substitute number in case she had to be absent one day. I responded by saying I had a feeling she was never out. She said, "I've missed one day in thirty years, and that's because my plane got delayed on my way back from a friend's daughter's weekend wedding. I'm never doing that again. If the wedding's out of town and not during summer break, I send gifts. I'm still mad at Delta for it." Just as we were passing the parking lot, several students approached her, anxious about an upcoming test. My day was done. Hers still wasn't over. Speaking to her students, she had clicked fully into teacher mode. Not wanting to disturb her, I headed toward my car without a word. A few seconds later she yelled after me, "Good luck this week!" I said "thanks" and held up a playful Huey Newton fist. "Kids' rights!" She waved at me with a grimace and walked toward her class, students in tow.

The notion of kids' rights isn't an idle one in education. During my year I often found myself teaching a class of absolutely rowdy middle schoolers, threatening to keep them in for recess if they didn't stop cutting up. They would turn to me indignantly and say I couldn't take recess away because they had "a right to play." Then they'd promptly go back to ignoring everything else I had to say and goof off for the remainder of class. And they were absolutely right. Tons of schools, charter and public, won't allow a teacher to deny a student recess for misbehaving because doing so, in the schools' eyes, violates their rights. When I told my younger brother about that, he was in shock. "I never saw the good outdoors during seventh grade, because I was held in for lunch so much," he told me. Same with me. Yet a school administrator reprimanded me for keeping a kid in during the fifteen-minute morning break after he threw an eraser across the room in my general direction. His classmates came to the door and said, "You not supposed to be doing this, mister. He can play if he wants." They then told the administrator, who came into the classroom and told the kid to go to recess and chastised me. I explained that he had thrown an eraser at me. She said, "Then we will deal with that, but our children have a right to their free time." When sixth-graders know their rights but don't know long division, or how to sit still and work when an adult tells them to, the school system has a problem.

Maybe you feel warm and fuzzy when you hear about someone championing kids' rights, as if they are finally defending kids against the awful tyranny of adults who would deny their right to the monkey bars just because they threw an eraser at someone. If so, you've not been paying attention to the world around you. The woman yelling about kids' rights on the radio was my first clue to how to unravel the puzzle of why that kid at Cullen got barely a slap on the wrist for cursing at me. Honoring kids' rights even in the face of serious misbehavior was becoming nearly commonplace in the toughest U.S. schools. And the idea didn't even start here. It started three thousand miles away, in Germany. You need to know about it.

Summerhill Academy was a city on a hill, actually a mountain in Hellerau, a suburb of Dresden, and later in Sonntagberg, Austria. The tiny school was a child's utopia. The lucky inmates were running the asylum. The Scottish education reformer Alexander S. Neill had founded his dream school in the aftermath of World War I and eventually moved it to England, then Wales, and finally back to the south of England after World War II.[1] There he set about the task of extending the full complement of human freedoms to children, the last population denied such rights by a corrupt world. Neill designed his school without an overseer, demands, or expectations. The individual happiness of each student, no matter how young, was all that mattered.

By the time he started Summerhill, Neill was a committed socialist and rested every human evil at the feet of social forces. "A criminal cannot help himself," he once wrote. "Heredity and environment make a man good or bad. . . . If a man is a murderer he is not responsible for his actions." Neill had become the twentieth century's most ardent acolyte of Rousseau's dictum that "man is born free but is everywhere in chains." Neill believed society's age-old methods of educating the young were the forger of those chains. Summerhill Academy would break the chains. In Neill's utopic vision, "no boy would learn to read a word until he desired to read; no boy would do anything unless he wanted to do it."[2]

Not many people would agree with this philosophy today, but at the time Neill's approach to education made him an international celebrity. His book *Summerhill: A Radical Approach to Child Rearing* (1960, with a foreword by Erich Fromm) became a best-seller in the United States. His writing and lecture tours provided the world with a look at what life was like in this British children's paradise. *Newsweek*, *Time*, and *The New York Times* all found column inches to devote to him. He even drew powerful detractors, including the famed anthropologist Margaret Mead. But Neill's liberationist notion of children's rights and freedoms had taken deep hold in the West. At a meeting of education reformers in the United States, no less a radical than the Black Panther Huey Newton called for a "human standard to arm kids with [to make them] free to determine their own lives."[3]

If Neill was the first of many brains behind the notion of children's rights, the United Nations was becoming the muscle. In 1923 activists, inspired by the appalling conditions children had suffered during World War I, began to press the League of Nations to institute global standards for the health and safety of children. This was the protectionist side of children's rights come to life, with advocates calling for a child's right to be fed, sheltered, educated, and, even more movingly, to be given a name. After the League was replaced by the United Nations, the effort cycled in and out of favor before culminating in the 1989 UN treaty called the Convention on the Rights of the Child. Its provisions are powerfully protectionist, including bans on child soldiers, child pornography, and sex trafficking. But some other provisions may surprise you:

> Article 13: The child shall have the right to freedom of expression; this right shall include freedom to seek, receive and impart information and ideas of all kinds, regardless of frontiers, either orally, in writing or in print, in the form of art, or through any other media of the child's choice.

> Article 14: States Parties shall respect the right of the child to freedom of thought, conscience and religion.

When the treaty was put before the entire UN body for a vote, it was ratified by 190 countries, becoming the most ratified treaty in UN history. But those who objected wanted to know: What does it mean for children to have the right to practice their own religion? How many millions of parents have dragged their kids out of bed, stuffed them into their best clothes, and hauled them to religious services? What does it mean for kids to have a right to express themselves? Does this mean a parent can't tell a kid to shut the hell up while they're trying to watch TV? Exactly these unanswered questions led Congress to reject the treaty, making the United States one of only three nations to do so (the others, Somalia and South Sudan, were not great company to be sure).[4]

The expansion of children's rights, typified by Summerhill and the UN, is what led the Harvard legal scholar Martha Minnow to declare that "advocates for children use the same rights . . . to place them in the same legal category as adults."[5] What does a thirty-year-old UN treaty that the United States has never ratified have to do with the day-to-day functioning of a school in a tough neighborhood, where kids refused to simply do as they were told? Where they are more aware of their newly conferred human rights than even the adults teaching them are? You might be interested to read Article 31 of the treaty:

> States Parties recognize the *right* of the child to rest and leisure, to engage in *play* and recreational activities appropriate to the age of the child and to participate freely in cultural life and the arts.

There it is: the right to play. Those rowdy middle schoolers were right. As of this writing, legislators in California are trying to pass a children's rights bill similar to the UN treaty, enshrining at the state level what Congress refused to thirty years ago.

But this was only part of what brought the toughest public schools in the country to the state at which I entered them just a few years ago. The elevation of children to the legal category of adults by international fiat, even if not ratified by the United States, was about to confront a social and cultural phenomenon that would wreak similar though infinitely more devastating havoc in the poorest pockets of U.S. inner cities. The combined power of these two forces would tear through the landscape and permanently alter for the worse the relationship between adult and child.

During the forty years between World War II and the mid-1980s, life for black Americans improved along every measurable social index available. With the advent of civil rights legislation especially, life expectancy, infant mortality, and income all were coming into closer alignment with those same measures of the white mainstream in the United States. The economic and structural supports for working- and middle-class life in the black community seemed to finally be taking permanent hold. But then the destruction of agricultural and manufacturing jobs after the war hit black inner cities especially hard, with a dramatic loss of employment. Into this world came a scourge, crack cocaine. A man named Rick Ross happened across a tiny rock-like substance that would make him one of the richest and most powerful criminal gangsters in American history. Someone had found a way to take a tiny amount of pure cocaine, mix it with water and baking soda, and, on an ordinary kitchen stove, produce crack. Cheap and powerful, with a high that reached the brain in only a matter of seconds, it made zombies of its users and laid waste to black homes and black families like nothing before it. It is important to acknowledge the widespread belief that crack was deliberately pumped into the inner city by the federal government to fund unauthorized and illegal activities abroad. And whether one is a conspiracist or not, it is easy to see where the belief came from. The impact on inner cities was near total.

The economist Steven Levitt has written that black American achievement was "hurt more by crack cocaine than any other single cause since Jim Crow." Michelle Alexander, in her book *The New Jim Crow*, remarked, "No one should ever attempt to minimize the harm caused by crack cocaine and the related violence . . . [it] 'blew through America's poor black neighborhoods like the Four Horsemen of the Apocalypse.'"[6] Poor inner cities, already dealing with the havoc of joblessness, fell into almost complete collapse. The homicide rate quadrupled, the black infant mortality rate soared (along with low birthrates and parental abandonment), the achievement gap between black and white students reversed its decline, stretching wider, and the number of blacks sent to prison more than tripled. Violence in schools of course took off too, as gang and turf wars spilled into the public schools and plunged them into chaos. (The "zero tolerance" policy of the 1990s grew out of those violent days.)[7] But even with all that, students were not yet fighting their teachers.

I began to understand that particular shift as I was driving home after a brutal day at a school in South LA. I was listening to the rebroadcast of an interview with someone who had been there at its creation: Shawn Carter, aka Jay-Z, the former-drug-dealer-turned-rap-impresario. Asked on NPR how the introduction of crack affected the neighborhood in which he grew up, he mentioned neither gang fights nor homicide rates nor police violence. He said, instead, something I'd never heard before:

> It changed the authority figure, because, you know, with crack cocaine it was done so openly. And the people who were addicted to it, the fiends, had very little self-respect. . . . It was so highly addictive that they didn't care how they obtained it. And they carried that out in front of children, who were dealing at the time. So that relationship of that respect—of, you know, I have to respect my elders and, you know, Uncle Tyrone's coming, who wasn't really your uncle, but he was the uncle for the neighborhood. And, you know, that dynamic shifted. And it had broke forever, and it just changed everything from that point on.[8]

I was so stunned by this that I nearly crashed into the car in front of me. Few cities were harder hit by crack cocaine than Los Angeles, where it was first manufactured and first worked its way into gang culture. Without knowing any details (my small town in the South was not heavily impacted by hard drugs) or experience to confirm what Jay-Z had said, it, nevertheless, felt unmistakably like the truth. It must've been something unnatural, I thought, something foreign and corrupting to reorder the very nature of black communal life so drastically. Devastatingly mind-altering and powerfully addictive, crack swept through poor communities like a biblical plague, leaving chaos and devastation in its wake. (Jay-Z wrote in his book *Decoded*: "No one hired a skywriter and announced crack's arrival. But when it landed in your hood, it was a total takeover. Sudden and complete. . . . What had been was gone, and in its place was a new way of life that was suddenly everywhere and seemed like it had been there forever.")[9]

During the next few days, as I thought through what I'd heard, I realized that Jay-Z had said so much in his brief remarks. It was clear to me that when a football player calls an adult well over twice his age a stupid motherfucker, threatens to fight him, and no one blinks an eye, the communal authority figure has changed. A Rubicon has been crossed. The kids in the toughest, poorest inner-city communities, kids who believed they no longer had any reason to respect the jobless and drug-ravaged adults, had gone from fighting each other to fighting the teachers.

Even now, the simple phrase from Jay-Z's radio interview, "crack cocaine was done so openly," resonates with me. As I am rewriting this chapter in my mom's house in the South, I've only just come from the gas station, where people were lined up to buy liquor. At first I wasn't sure what they were doing; I thought they were buying lottery tickets. Then they emerged with cans wrapped in brown paper bags. I hadn't seen that in almost twenty years. All my life, and that of any adult African American older than, say, thirty-five, who grew up in a black neighborhood, the sign that an adult was drinking alcohol was the brown paper bag that hid the alcohol from the view of the public and particularly children. The drinker might be sitting on a porch with his nieces and nephews or having a cookout with family, but he always kept the liquor hidden (in plain sight). When an adult was drinking in public, society drew a line between publicly acceptable behavior and less publicly acceptable behavior, between the adult world and the child world, and the brown paper bag was the evidence of that line. Kids would put their soda cans in brown paper bags to pretend they were drinking liquor and then of course hurriedly discard the bag if an adult walked by. But crack was so devastating in its effects that it upended the basic social compact about what could be done in public, in front of children, and what should be hidden. From *Decoded*:

> Doing coke was something that happened at private parties, something you might've heard about but had never really seen. Crackheads were different. They'd smoke in hallways, on playgrounds,

on subway station staircases. They got no respect. They were former neighbors, "aunts" and "uncles," but once they started smoking, they were simply crackheads. . . . They had no secrets.[10]

But, it should be said, this was more than just a social transformation. It was an economic transformation too. The crack economy was, in essence, a child's economy. The adult gang members who controlled the trade in LA and other major cities quickly realized that children were exempt from the harsh mandatory sentences meted out to adult dealers. After less than a year in juvenile detention, a child could be back hustling on the street; kids constituted a readily recycled labor force. This was a sea change, and it unsettled even black law enforcement. "I grew up here," a Detroit-area law enforcement officer told *Time* magazine in 2001. "There were drugs in our neighborhood. But they were heroin dealers. They didn't mess with children. That was the difference." The adults who controlled the crack economy were the first to traduce the boundary between adult and child. In Washington, DC, juvenile drug arrests increased from 483 in 1983 to 1,894 in 1987, just four short years. Police also made thirty-five drug arrests of kids younger than twelve that year. Four years earlier they had made none. *Time* described the amount of money the most successful kids in the drug trade were suddenly making:

Lookout (9–10 year olds)	Can earn up to $100 a day warning dealers when police are in the area. Youngest ones often rewarded with the most fashionable sneakers or a bike.
Runner	Up to $300 a day transporting the drugs from the makeshift factories where the cocaine is cooked into crack.
Dealer	The best, most enterprising dealers in a hot market can make up to $3,000 a week.[11]

When I was a child, adults shielded kids from even the sight of publicly consumed alcohol, but the control crack had over its users was so great that, much like the opioid users of today, they surrendered the traditional constraints that shielded kids from illicit adult behavior. Further, the crack epidemic brought children as young as ten into the heart of a violent underground economy and made many of them financially independent of adults. "I wasn't even a teenager yet and suddenly everyone I knew had pocket money. And better," Jay-Z writes. "Guys my age [fifteen], fed up watching their moms struggle on a single income, were paying utility bills with money from hustling. So how could those same mothers sit them down about a truant report?"[12]

If you doubt how universal the dramatic psychological effect is on children who have demonstrated more earning power than their parents, here is what the former supermodel Christy Turlington Burns said of her life in fashion: "I started working so young, my order in my family definitely changed because of what I was earning. I became equal to my father very early . . . that was always my goal. Of course men and women are equal; growing up, I thought my father had so much more autonomy and power. I wanted those characteristics and qualities."[13] Turlington had entered the world of high fashion when she was thirteen and never looked back. Before she was old enough to vote, the money she was earning made her "as powerful" as her father and made her his equal. The money earned by the children of the crack economy did the same for them, as they enjoyed the money and glamour that came with being a dealer or a runner or a lookout in the only economic game in town available to them. Add to this the ritual humiliations to which the powerfully addicted adults could not help but subject themselves to in front of the teens and preteens who were dealing, and you have a world in which the natural relationship between adult and child was fatefully severed. As one commentator I overheard said, "Nothing could stop black mothers from mothering. Not slavery. Not segregation. But crack cocaine could." The center of black life in the inner cities simply could not hold.

The actress Jada Pinkett Smith described what it was like growing up as the daughter of a drug addict at the height of Baltimore's crack epidemic. "Oh man, I wonder what I'm going to eat tonight because there's no food here. How am I going to get to school? And is my mom going to be okay today? Will this be one more day she survives her addiction? That's the kind of stuff I had to think about at 12."[14] The feeling of being abandoned by the adults of a completely transformed world was real. The New York rapper Biggie Smalls says in his song "Things Done Changed," "Back in the days, our parents used to take care of us / Look at 'em now, they even fuckin scared of us." For his part, the rapper Tupac Shakur, the son of a crack addict, coined the acronym T.H.U.G. L.I.F.E.: The Hate U Give Little Infants Fucks Everyone.

Thus the general evolution in the West of the children's rights movement, which "placed children in the same legal positions as adults," joined with the dreadful effects of a youth-driven drug economy to destroy the traditional domestic life of millions of poor inner-city kids. It should come as no surprise, then, that this lethal admixture was also fatal to the orderly and healthy functioning of the institutions—schools and churches—charged with helping to raise those children. The natural order of things had been turned on its head. As I tried to absorb the impact of these twin phenomena, the only thing I could liken it to was a bizarre phantasmagoria: it was as if the world's oceans were gradually warming because of the effects of climate change, only to have a thousand fire-breathing dragons descend from the sky and set the seas boiling with fire. It was an apocalypse.

I knew none of this when I started working in schools because no one tells you. Late in my year of subbing, I asked a sophomore (not the football player I discussed in the introduction) whether he had done his homework. From across the room, he erupted, pounding his fist into his hand and walking toward me in a rage, unaccountably angry and threatening me with a fight. "What you gon' do? What you gon' do? We can handle this now. We both grown men. We both grown men." He was fifteen. This was a world in which the balance of power had shifted.

There had been warning signs. And some had heeded them. Teachers. Veteran teachers, many black, some white, who had taught in these schools for ages but were now the harried scapegoats for the failures of society at large. These veterans were the last vestiges of communal authority in our nation's toughest schools. They were the Guardians of the North, derided and disbelieved but hewing to their duty to warn the nation that the world was collapsing beneath their feet. Today, the worst of the crack epidemic and the attendant violence seems over, but its aftermath lives on. The children of this apocalypse eventually grew up, and, as night follows day, had children of their own. It was these children who I was seeing day in and day out in some of the poorest schools in Los Angeles—confused, resentful, hilarious, tender, and angry— struggling to learn and grow and escape the legacy of a world they didn't create.

But if the darkest shadow has now passed beyond the inner cities, the Four Horsemen have once again found their steeds and pointed them inward, toward America's heartland. The opioid crisis is sweeping through the Midwest today with the same ferocity that the crack epidemic engulfed inner cities thirty years ago, and the joblessness and despair that such a crisis feeds on show no sign of waning. If the schools and churches of the white working class have not yet felt the impact of this devastation, they soon will. Perhaps the pages that follow, tough and bracing though they may be, can help point a way forward not just for the black and Latin youth I encountered every day, but the poor whites a world away.

I end this chapter, then, with a question: What is it like for teachers teaching in the aftermath of an apocalypse? It can be life-affirming and hysterical and completely transformative. But mostly it is very hard. Sometimes impossible. Yet many still try. But for the teacher heading for the first time into schools where the authority figures have vanished, a better question might be: What does it sound like?

through the classwork and get Junior to talk about something besides pussy. Whatever she was reading on her phone sent her into bursts of laughter, which she shared with her friends and boyfriend, setting them laughing too.

I'd been subbing at this point for a little more than two weeks, and I'd gotten a sense of how this works. The kids knew I'd be there for two days, and they were trying to see what I was made of: whether I was scared of them and someone they could walk over or whether I could "get it crackin'." I wanted them to think of me as someone who could always "get it crackin'."

In international relations there is a concept called the monopoly of power, and whatever entity has the most power over a physical territory has the monopoly. In the United States, the federal government has the monopoly over U.S. territory. When there's a real challenge to that monopoly, you've got an insurgency or perhaps a civil war on your hands. Each time I stood in front of a new group of kids, I was determined to discourage either from happening, to hold on to the monopoly as long as I could. But this girl was testing me. Although I had twice asked her to sit down and put her phone away, she was still texting, telling me to "hold up" each time. My general rule was the standard three strikes. So I asked again. She replied, "I said, 'Hold up.'" When a child of thirteen or fourteen, or of any age for that matter, says something to me like "I said, 'Hold up,'" the quick flash of anger that courses through my brain is hard to describe. I never came to view this as a bad thing, though I'm sure education theorists will say you shouldn't ever get angry at kids. That's nonsense. Instead I took that flash of red as a sign that my brain was still working properly. I simply tamped it down and focused it into my most black-kid-who-grew-up-in-the-rural-South-and-had-tough-black-parents-and-tough-teachers voice and simply said, "It ain't gonna be a whole lot more 'hold ups' in this class. What's about to happen is you're about to get on out of here." By the time the dust cleared, both she and her boyfriend, Rodiney, had cursed at me, and I had kicked them both out of the classroom.

I didn't know or really care where the campus aide took them, but at the bell I sat at the desk and tried to settle myself. Even winning a quarrel with a kid can rattle you, especially since I sort of liked all the kids I'd met. It was a rare occasion for me to meet a kid I thought was truly incorrigible or irredeemable, even though many would push my patience beyond the breaking point. There was a fifteen-minute break before the start of third period, so I decided to run to the bathroom before the break was over, and as I moved into the hall I passed the throng of kids, and it dawned on me what that hum back at City High was. The quiet, persistent, distinguishing hum was the sound of a bunch of kids talking, yelling, laughing, having fun. But something was missing that made the hum at City High seem quieter, even if it actually wasn't. The kids at Cullen were talking and yelling and having fun too, but they were also cursing. The kids at City High didn't curse, not within my earshot at least, and I started to realize that that distinction—not within my earshot—mattered. I was still getting used to this world, trying to see where the cracks and the clues and the map to surviving it were, and audible cursing was one of them. I don't mean Junior's somewhat comical swearing, and definitely not the cursing aimed directly at me; it was the cursing *around* me. As I walked past students at Cullen, they were casually cursing in the halls, unperturbed that an adult more than twice their age could hear them clearly.

From that moment in my second week it was clear: if I walked through the front door of a school and heard kids swearing as I walked past, and they kept swearing, I was in for a rough day. If I walked into a tough school and saw them blush when they realized I'd heard them, I knew I'd be okay. It was the most pervasive sign that the world Jay-Z had described—the one where things were once hidden between generations, and lines of intergenerational respect and authority were still in place—no longer really existed. Hearing children curse *in the presence of adults* is the "broken windows" of public education: the tiny outward sign that a school (and the community that it inhabited) was in trouble.[1] Check the school's math scores—they're always low; check its reading scores— they're in the tank. Cursing around adults is the visible (or auditory) evidence of a collapsed school and community environment, where emotional chaos dominates a child's day.

This was not just my whimsical litmus test. A complex and interesting science studies a child's use of curse words. Cursing is a natural stage in a child's development, not at all unlike lying. And the latest research on lying suggests it is "a developmental milestone . . . a reassuring sign that [a child's] cognitive growth is intact."[2] As kids begin to develop interest in their corporeal self— the sexual and bodily functions that accompany a human's daily life—they also take an innocent interest in the crudest words for those functions. David, a friend of mine, told me a funny story about his seven-year-old son, Adam, who leaned into him quietly one day and said, "Dad, I know the s-word." David waited in horror. Adam whispered, "Stupid." My friend nodded, relieved. Adam continued, "I know the c-word." Again, David tensed. His son leaned in and said, "Can't." Second bullet dodged. But later that year, while on a family vacation, David and Adam were watching a Billy Crystal stand-up special. At some point the camera zoomed in on Crystal's face. "Fuck you," Crystal said, straight to the camera. Adam exploded: "That's the f-word!" The fateful day had arrived: the knowledge of good and evil could no longer be postponed.

This kind of thing happens a million times a day every day. And during my time as a sub I logged plenty of examples of the "developmental," and largely forgivable, use of swearing. I subbed for a day at an Orthodox Jewish school and was assigned to the girls' part of the school, but halfway through the day I was asked to cover a class of all boys. I said sure. By the time I got there, word had spread that a six-foot-three black guy in a baseball cap (my version of the yarmulke the male teachers were wearing) was in the building. When I walked in to relieve the teacher, the boys erupted in excitement, with three of them playfully doing the hora. The teacher, surprised, asked whether I had taught them before. I told the truth: it was my first day and I'd never seen them before. It was near the end of the period, and the teacher had given them free time for the remainder of the class. Some were on their computers, others read books, still others were huddled over one gaming system or another. I told them the usual rules, especially "no salty language," and left them to their fun. At some point I heard someone loudly say "pussy fart." I glanced in the offender's direction. The scared look on one boy's face told me who it was. In a pointed voice I asked, "What was that?" His friend's eyes darted back and forth, making clear he hoped to not be caught in the line of fire. The guilty party spoke up nervously: "Nothing." I stared a little longer and he cowered, not sure what I'd do next. "Okay," I responded slowly. "Let's make sure we keep it that way." They were seventh-grade boys and I knew hormones controlled every aspect of their minds, but their fear of my wrath (healthily expressed by lying to me) was the proper response. Just like their interest in pussy farts. So I let it pass and went back to surfing the internet.

A somewhat different experience unfolded shortly after that in a class of kindergartners at a Conservative Jewish school where the boys and girls learned together. I was the coteacher that day. The students had broken up into small groups, and I was working with about six kids on a matching worksheet. Jessica, all of five years old and sitting right next to me, said, "Hey, mister, I know a bad word." I looked at her. "It rhymes with *sit*." I was not sure where she was going with this and just stared at her. "And I can spell it," she added. Before I could think to stop her, she started in: "*S-h-*"

I interrupted, "Hey, hey, Jessica, we're not spelling new words right now. We're matching, okay?"

"Okay, but I know how to spell it," she insisted.

I assured her that I believed her, but I didn't need her to prove it right there in Temple Beth Jerusalem's kindergarten, so I just pointed to her worksheet and tried to get her back on task. But I wasn't out of the woods yet, because Jessica's spelling had apparently awakened Abaranne, also five, who was pretty much ignoring her work and mouthing the word *fuck* over and over to her classmates. Jessica enjoined her: "You're not supposed to be saying that, Abaranne." But Abaranne kept at it. *Fuck-fuck-fuck-fuck-fuck.* I was thrown. She wasn't saying it out loud exactly, and my mind had locked up. I hadn't expected this, so I didn't think to say, "Stop saying that right now." I also didn't want to alert the other students to what she was saying because they were pretty much ignoring her. Then Abaranne added some volume to her voice and said *fuck* directly into the ear of a girl who pushed her away with a grimace. I finally came to and said, "Abaranne, I need you to stop that and do your work. You're bothering your classmates." The mean look she gave me seemed to involve at least one curse word.

But as I keyed in on Abaranne, I noticed she didn't seem quite like the other kids. She had not completed any of her work; her coloring had none of the control of her other classmates', her handwriting was impossible to decipher, and nearly all her math problems were incomplete or wrong. She also had taken off her shoes and was walking around barefoot on the cool floor. I was curious about her and casually mentioned to the teacher during the transition to recess that Abaranne hadn't finished her work. "Yeah, that's Abaranne," she said a bit wearily. "She's different." Needless to say, I have no formal training in the complex world of child neurological development, and surely don't want to overstate the facts, but this assignment came at the end of December and I'd subbed in about a half-dozen classes of kindergartners by then, enough to think her behavior suggested that she might have some developmental issues. Mouthing the word *fuck* over and over in class at age five was only part of it.

I do think, however, it was easy to diagnose Abaranne with a lack of impulse control; that may have been the manifestation of a more deeply rooted issue, but the lack of control seemed clear. We know enough about the fundamental qualities needed for academic (and professional) achievement to know that impulse control is central to success. Abaranne wanted to take her shoes off in class and walk around barefoot, so she did. She wanted to color outside the lines of a drawing even at five, so she did. She wanted to say the harshest swear word she knew, so she did, repeatedly. Abaranne couldn't control her impulses for reasons I was unaware of, and the adults rearing her had not found a way to help her. That her academic achievement was also apparently low was no surprise. Jessica struggled with the impulse to say bad words in a healthy manner, knowing it was wrong (she called it a "bad word"), and chose to spell it rather than say it. The boys at the Orthodox school had impulse control but slipped because their teacher was out of the room and the cool sub had come in, and they unconsciously relaxed those controls. The look I gave them told them to go back to un-relaxing those controls and they did.

The other example of normal cursing was "p-word" Junior at Cullen. It skirted a type of danger, I believe, but was largely a mixture of impulse and something more developmental. That developmental part is best illustrated by another Junior from the TV show *The Sopranos*. In the pilot episode, Tony, the don of New Jersey, is at home with his wife, Carmela. It's the birthday of their son, Tony Jr. After a few scenes depicting Tony Sr.'s bloody profession, laced with all the profanity we've come to expect from an Italian mobster, the episode cuts to the evening of the boy's birthday party. Visitors are slowly arriving, including the local priest, who has a crush on Carmela. Young Tony enters the scene with bad news: his grandmother, purveyor of an apparently deli-cious baked ziti, won't be attending. After the adults jabber irrita-bly among themselves, Junior, pudgy and barely five feet tall, the only kid standing among the grown-ups, suddenly interjects, "So, what? No fucking ziti now?" The adults react in instant and an-gry unison: "Hey!" "Hey!" "Whoa!" The priest smacks him on the backside and the scene ends. Even foul-mouthed mobsters don't tolerate children cursing in their presence.

Tony Jr. did not suffer from a lack of impulse control in that moment. He was deliberately testing, at age thirteen, the line be-tween him and the adult world around him. And all the adults, though very different in their roles and natures (one a priest, one a mob boss), uniformly and quickly reinforced the line. P-word Junior was testing the adult-child boundary in a hilarious way, but he also sometimes had questionable impulse control, like all teens. In tough schools cursing represents both a lack of impulse control and a type of aggression against the adult world, and the mob bosses and priests have stopped trying to clamp down. For this reason, the wave of swear words I heard every day, well within my earshot, starting in middle schools, felt like a frontal assault. As if the kids were saying they were every bit as grown as I was, and there was nothing I was going to do about it.

The power that taboo words have over us is, as the psycholo-gist Steven Pinker has noted, their ability to "evoke an emotional response in an audience against their wishes."[3] Having kids curse at and around you with no consequences is to feel yourself out of control. It gnawed at my sense of right and wrong, and it rattled me. Hearing kids regularly say "fuck" and "shit" while you're ex-plaining fractions makes your mind think of fucking and shitting and makes it hard to focus on cross-multiplying. But it had be-come commonplace at some schools. Apparently several years after I stopped subbing at Cullen, the administration started buying pizza for the kids if they didn't curse at a teacher that day. Times are tough for teachers.

To illustrate how drastically the world that black kids are growing up in has changed in a generation (though not what it means to be a child), lyrics by the rapper Common describe an emblematic scene that played out in every black household across the country in 1988, after the hip-hop and R&B group Guy came out with the song "Piece of My Love." Common described going to an amusement park with his girlfriend while they were dressed in the same outfits.

> Round then Guy came out with "Piece of My Love"
> Arguin' over if he said, "Dumb bitch"[4]

Thirty years ago, hearing someone curse in a song was so shocking and so foreign that Common and his friends in Chicago (where today the murder rate is among the highest in the nation), and my siblings and I in a small town in the South, were stunned at the possibility that the lead singer of Guy might have called a girl a bitch on a record. It was just unfathomable to us that that language barrier would have been crossed. (Many people are old enough to remember their parents shooing kids out of the room to listen to Richard Pryor and George Carlin records in private. Like the brown paper bag covering the liquor bottle, the closed door through which you could hear the grown-ups laughing at a comedian's muffled adult humor was a boundary the adults enforced.) Times have changed. The crack epidemic (and the rights of children) changed it.

That was why I became obsessed with stopping kids from cursing around me. And trying to eliminate or minimize it in any class I covered. I'd recite an opening spiel in each class and eventually say, "I have just one absolute rule. No salty language. If you just got to curse somebody out today, send them a text, slide into their DMs, post it on Facebook, something, I just don't want to hear it." They'd laugh, and we'd get on with the day. If I heard someone curse (and I always heard many someones), I'd look at them, arch an unfriendly eyebrow, and say, "Watch your language." If they cursed again, I'd stare at them hard, raise two fingers, and say, "That's the second time," and let it hang there. On the third time, they had to go stand in the hall for one minute as their classmates laughed at them getting kicked out. If they cursed me while leaving I jawed right back at them and told them to not come back until they had a pass from the office. This is exactly the exchange you want, and 80 percent of the time, if students in tough high schools saw me regularly, this worked. At the point at which students started to chastise each other for cursing in my class ("Watch your mouth around Mr. Henderson!"), or when one tenth-grader came to me and said, "Just kick me out now, Mr. Henderson, I ain't gonna be able to not curse today," I knew I had them, and one basic line of respect had been restored. If they cursed but I didn't hear it, it wasn't my business, and I didn't care. *But they would not do it around me.* It was a tiny but, I believe, necessary victory in a long battle to foster a healthy relationship between growing children and the adult world.

I want to raise another issue about why allowing kids to swear openly is troubling. The history of swear words suggests part of the reason. Curse words are some of the oldest and most tenacious words in use, activating the most buried and ancient parts of the human brain. *Fuck* as a description for intercourse is five hundred years old; *bitch*, which originally meant a lewd or sensual woman, is more than six hundred years old. *Cunt*, used to refer to a woman's genitalia, was first recorded more than eight hundred years ago, and *shit* quite likely was used by the preliterate Germanic clans of the Roman Empire.[5]

Recent research has shown that since the early twentieth

century a dramatic change has been taking place among young girls: they have been entering puberty earlier and developing faster than ever before. A generation ago, fewer than 5 percent of girls entered puberty before age eight, with puberty typically occurring between ages eight and thirteen; today the cohort that reaches puberty especially early has more than doubled. When the numbers are sifted for race, we see something even more alarming. Today a little more than 10 percent of Caucasian girls are growing breasts before the age of eight, whereas 15 percent of Latino girls do, and a staggering 25 percent of black girls begin sexual maturation at far earlier ages than their counterparts just twenty years ago. The researchers make a compelling case that three factors are responsible: obesity; chemicals found in the environment; and extrabiological factors, like childhood trauma, poor familial relations, and exposure to older peers and age-inappropriate media. They also note that girls who grow up without their biological father in the home (as the majority of poor black girls do) are twice as likely to develop a menstrual cycle before the age of eight. Research with boys suggests an earlier onset of puberty among them as well, with similarly unsettling racial disparities.[6]

In this internet age, when sexually graphic imagery pours out of every phone and radio and mobile device, "inappropriate media" are everywhere. And one anthropologist has written of cases in which men's regular and constant flirting with prepubescent girls has "accelerated the onset of [the menstrual cycle]."[7] In that vein, I've long thought that one of the causes of teenage pregnancy in areas of society, both black and white, where sexual desirability is a valued part of a girl's identity, for those girls who struggle with low self-image or believe themselves to be ugly, having a child is permanent and indisputable proof, to her and the world around her, that someone once found her sexually desirable. Adolescent pregnancy was often attributed to a girl wanting to have something to love; but it's just as possible that for some girls a baby is lasting evidence that she was once "loved" (desired) by someone. Even if no one ever sees the boy who desired her, the child is proof he did. My point is that lowering the sexual temperature around girls in schools is important to help them achieve, but removing the taboo around the use of the most sexually mature language available—which is what allowing adolescents to swear openly around adults does—helps in some small measure to keep that temperature high.

I had not read any of this research on puberty or sexuality and kids when I first walked into a classroom. I just knew that something was wrong with seventh-graders or tenth-graders (or Abaranne) saying "fuck" around me.

But this was just a little bucket in a seemingly bottomless sea. What of the other broken windows? The now notorious police practice punished even the smallest infraction at the point of a gun, and the practice has led to the shocking and sickening murders of black men at the hands of law enforcement. How does the senseless killing of Eric Garner at the hands of a cop and George Zimmerman's acquittal in the killing of Trayvon Martin, and the powerful Black Lives Matter movement that erupted out of it, connect to what is going on in our public schools? It took a lot more time to figure out. In the meantime, other, more confounding, mysteries were mounting.

As for Junior, that kid was hopeless. And too funny to make any of my anger stick. Even if he didn't say the p-word, he'd write "*I love pussy*" on his classwork and turn it in. I'd hand it back to him and say I wouldn't grade it until he erased it. He'd erase it, hand it back to me, and say, "But I still love it." Finally I hatched a plan. After one class I kept him in my room and asked him if he liked scary movies. He said, "Yeah." "Yeah," I told him, "people like being scared. Another word for *scared* is *pusillanimous*. Why don't you say that instead of the word you like saying? And it's a college-level word. People will see how smart you are."

He grinned. "Pussy-lanimous," he said.

I corrected him. "Puss-i-lanimous."

"Pussy-lanimous," he repeated.

I wasn't going to win this. "Get out, Junior," I told him. As he walked out, he asked, "Is that why they say somebody is being a pussy if they scared?" I hadn't thought of that. "Yeah, maybe so," I said.

"Cool, I love me some pussy-lanimous," he said as he exited into the hall.

3

Gems, Knuckleheads, and Assholes

Some kids you take at their word. They give you a look or issue a type of ultimatum and you're inclined to go along with them. They're not chaotic or unpredictable, but you sense they're capable of being both. The bargain they offer is sometimes implied, sometimes stated outright. When it's explicit, they're not doing it to draw attention to themselves or to cause trouble. It's simply that they're clear about where they stand in the world, and they want to make it clear to you too. You can accept or reject the bargain, but know that if you reject it, good luck. They usually have friends close by.

That was David. I liked him from the start. He was Latino, one of the tallest students at Cullen, an easy six feet, built heavy but not fat, like a solid block. When I first met him during my first few days subbing there, he was in an eleventh-grade honors class I was teaching. He casually said to me as I handed out the worksheet for kids to complete, "Hey mister, don't try and get me to do no work, okay?" Until that day, I'd never had a kid say something like that to me. I'd have kids say much worse. I'd have kids knock the work off the desk, tell me they weren't doing shit, and slide the sheet over to another student while ignoring me as I passed by them. But this was different.

I said, "What?" He repeated himself, without changing his tone, "Don't try and get me to do no work. Okay?" Then, seeing my confusion, he explained: "I won't bother you. I'm just gonna sit here and draw." I looked at the drawing of what seemed to be a very futuristic car, then back at him. He was calmly staring at me. I promptly collected the worksheet I'd put in front of him, said, "Cool car," and moved on to the next kid. It was a wise decision.

Other students want to fight you. From the first moment you meet them, they've got you in their crosshairs. You mean nothing to them and they have every intention of letting you know that. But they're not actually trouble, as hard as it may be to tell in the middle of them talking recklessly to you. Kids like that are goading you because they want to see what you're capable of. It's pure brinksmanship, but they actually want you to win. It's in your best interest to go at them as hard as they come at you, because they're testing whether they can trust you. The fight they put up asks important questions: Are you really an adult? Are you fair? Do you see me? Are you tough enough to keep us safe? *I hope so*, they are telling you, *because adults have been missing from this place for a long time.*

So a student named Clarice tried me, until she didn't. She was also hilariously funny and had, since the age of six, whupped everyone she ever met, man, woman, or child, at Connect Four. I played her twice and each time the game was over before I'd even realized what had happened. I spent the year trying to get a rematch and salvage my dignity but she refused, waving me off, bored and irritated that she'd even played me in the first place.

Still other students will never even attempt to try you. That was Greg and Dayshawn. Together those two formed a self-reinforced peer group that wielded great power at Cullen. Dayshawn was massive, an athlete and in AP classes. Greg was his ebullient sidekick and wherever they went a halo of goodness preceded them and followed in their wake. During Halloween they came fully dressed as X-Men. They wore red Santa caps for the entire month of December. Trouble avoided them, and they had a keen eye for suffering. The disabled kids who were all taught in one class were their biggest fans. One kid, Brian, who was confined to a wheelchair, had had his Cullen shirt signed by Dayshawn the day after a big game. It was his prized possession. If Brian was in the hall and Dayshawn was too, Dayshawn would find his way to wherever Brian was, and together with Greg, the three of them spread goodwill and comity to everyone.

Demetrius was somewhere in the middle, a loner, a satellite lurking away from the rest of the planets. He allied himself most closely with David, a rarity, as black and Latino kids rarely hung out together. But they shared a passion: they liked to fight. David had been dubbed Dr. Sleep by a teacher because he had knocked four people out cold. David and Demetrius bonded over a weekend when they found themselves on the same crosstown bus, heading to fight boys from a rival housing project. David ended up knocking out one of the kids. When Demetrius dropped out of Cullen, his girlfriend soon followed, but then she showed up in class a few days later. Demetrius had sent her back to school, saying, "If we're gonna be together we can't both be dummies." I loved Demetrius.

There was Rodiney, of course. Moody, troubled, and easily swayed by the company he kept in the moment he was keeping it, but fundamentally a good kid. He, like Junior, was susceptible to trouble but never really the cause of it.

And then there was Erik. He was a scoundrel. He wielded more power than all the other students combined. Not because he was stronger or more clever or tougher than David or Demetrius, or even Dayshawn for that matter. In fact, Erik managed to steer clear of all of them (bullies know who to test and who not to), while pressing the boundaries with the adults and kids who were scared of him. His older brother had been expelled for punching a female teacher and had fought a few male teachers before that; all had quit. Erik, it seemed, had taken on the role of two scoundrels now that his brother was no longer at the school. Yet nothing he did seemed to get him in trouble.

These, by and large, were the most memorable students I taught that year of subbing. And if I taught many more that year—and I did, well over ten thousand more, comprising every race, economic status, grade, and religion—they all had something in common. They fell into one of three categories. They were either gems, knuckleheads, or assholes. Sometimes they were two (it was rarely a fixed identity) and some could be all three. Of course these are purposefully crude distinctions, but they are instructive. Clarice was pure knucklehead, as were Rodiney and Junior. I came to love all three of them. Greg and Dayshawn, whom I adored, were the purest of gems. David (Dr. Sleep) and Demetrius may well have been assholes to some people, the kids they jumped or knocked out cold, but in my class they were gems. But Erik was a menace, a pure and unadulterated asshole. We, as adults, blanch at the idea that a kid can be a nasty human being—and, in fairness, with patience and love and proper discipline some rage-filled, violent kids can transform into beautiful gems—but there are some kids, some small percentage, for whom that transformation never happens. Erik was, to everyone, an unmitigated asshole. You name it: fights, threats, stealing, cursing teachers, attempting to fight teachers. He even aimed minor cruelties at a few of the kids with disabilities in the school. Toward the end of September, I heard a few teachers in the teacher's lounge saying that Erik was back. "Who's Erik?" I asked. If he's in your class, I was told, you'll know. He was eventually in my class.

Of the three types of students I described, the Eriks are the most powerful and the Dayshawns the least powerful, but the knuckleheads, the Juniors and Rodineys and Clarices, are the most important.

Knuckleheads are the kids who are well behaved when the kids around them are well behaved and cut-ups when the other kids are cut-ups. If there are mostly gems in the class, knuckleheads behave like gems. If too many kids are rowdy and aggressive—if there are one too many Eriks in the class, then the knuckleheads become like Eriks too. I realized rather quickly that the struggle for the soul of a troubled school is a struggle for the souls of the knuckleheads.

I believe these categories are not just confined to schools. I think they describe how all institutions work. Think of the Second Persian Gulf War. The three people responsible for pulling us into the most costly and consequential armed conflict of the last fifty years were Colin Powell, George W. Bush, and Dick Cheney. Powell was dead-set against the war from the start; Bush was on the fence, though already war-minded because of the 9/11 attacks; Cheney, however, was obsessed. He had "a fever" when it came to Saddam Hussein, according to reports at the time. And so, in the absence of a compelling case against the Iraqi dictator, Cheney helped mastermind one by distorting national intelligence and pillorying detractors, all in his headlong quest to persuade an easily swayed president (and nation) that the need for war was inexorable. By the time Cheney was through, he had managed to wield the levers of power with such cleverness that he forced Powell to permanently sully his reputation by going before the United Nations with falsified evidence and make Cheney's (and Bush's) case for war. In the years since, Bush and Powell have both expressed regret for sending the nation to war (and plunging the Middle East into chaos) under false pretenses. Cheney remains openly defiant, insisting he'd do it all over again if he could. Colin Powell, George W. Bush, Dick Cheney: gem, knucklehead, asshole.

In the writing of this book, I was surprised and gratified to learn that the hunch I'd developed—the crude g/k/a distinction—had basis in research. An organization called Turnaround for

Children, a nonprofit that was created to address the impact of trauma on students in public schools, found this:

> Many of the behavioral-management challenges that educators in high-poverty schools face are due to the combustible combination, in the classroom, of two cohorts of students. The first is a small group of students who . . . are angry and rebellious and disruptive. This group . . . represents between 10 and 15 percent of the student body in the most high-poverty schools. Students in the second cohort . . . are less likely to start trouble, but their highly sensitive fight-or-flight mechanisms are easily triggered when trouble comes.[1]

When one hears these statistics and one experiences, as I have many times, just this "combustible combination" of students, one can perhaps begin to understand why simple but important acts of stringency are necessary in the toughest schools, like being able to give detention or send a kid to the office, or, when necessary, suspend for a day or two, some of the 10 to 15 percent of the most angry and rebellious. But the ability to enforce these remedies has been all but stripped away from school administrators.

It is hard to describe how deeply disorienting it was to work in schools where this combustible combination exists, but no one (except the teachers) was willing to acknowledge, address, or manage it. It was bizarre and confusing to one day be summoned to a well-run middle- and upper-middle-class school where kids had to surrender their phones if they were merely caught with them even during passing period, let alone having them out in class, and then the very next day be sent to a school in East LA where a student who I'd been warned was notoriously tough pushed a pregnant teacher in order to grab a laptop from her because he wanted to watch a video, and when the dean came to address the issue, they asked the teacher what was going on because the kid seemed "not to be jibing with her."

Or to another middle school where a kid in my class was caught with a crack rock in his bag and sixth-grade girls talked and texted on their phones throughout class and cursed at me in the most aggressive way, and when I tried to chastise them, one of them called her dad to say I was bothering her and her friends and asked whether he could come up to school and handle me. (It was the last period of the day, and apparently her dad was a black belt in karate, so I hustled out of there at the end of school as fast as I could.) This was a school where several teachers had taken a leave of absence because they had been assaulted by students. When I asked two teachers who were sitting together during lunch what was up with the behavior and discipline system they laughed ruefully and said, "We're still working on getting one of those." It was also a school where a sixth-grader had to use fingers to add 20 and 70 and two other kids had to guess three times what 12 minus 8 was, and one of them used their fingers for that too. And another kid who wrote 500 when I asked the class to write the number 5 million.

I thought I was in the Twilight Zone and that I literally was seeing either the beginning or the end of the world. The most basic norms of up and down, left and right, inside and out seemed to be under some fundamental siege and I was helpless to understand it. As this happened over and over in my first few weeks—spending one day at a terrific, thriving school where there were clear boundaries and consequences for violating basic rules of respect between adults and kids, followed the next day at a school where kids could barely read and write but could openly curse and threaten you—my mind began to darken. Take that madhouse of a middle school where I was chastised for violating a kid's right to play. I was also told on another occasion that I couldn't send kids out or to the office. Instead, they let kids take their own break when the kid felt they needed one. "We like our kids to have autonomy," the thirtysomething white dean at this all-Latino school, where seventh-graders couldn't even do basic multiplication, told me. (This was the same dean who asked the pregnant teacher why things weren't jibing with her and the kid who pushed her.) When in the history of humanity has a middle school student, having the time of his life swinging from the rafters with his buddies while they all ignored their classwork, ever suddenly stopped and said to himself, "You know what? I'm having *too* much fun right now. Let me step into the hall and take a breather, then go back in and re-focus on the homework I didn't do last night." (That the teacher I was subbing for had abruptly quit due to exhaustion in the middle of the semester didn't seem to register with the administration.)

That so many of these schools and school districts were largely being administered by white people only made my mind darken more. What were they doing? Why were they giving these poor kids license to do any and everything they wanted to do? It would be one thing if they had instituted meaningful and effective alternatives to the normal stringent measures we all grew up with—if, instead of detention and suspension for a kid for cursing at a teacher, there was some deep and effective therapeutic alternative, some reformative system of counseling and healing to deal with angry or impulsive kids—but none of that existed in the nearly fifty schools I worked in either. Ever. It was just madness, time and again. There was never a response to the behavior of these troubled kids in the worst schools other than "Let's not call Ms. White a dumb bitch and throw her computer out the window again today, because that's not nice."

I am not conspiracy-minded. Tell me you think 9/11 was an inside job and my eyes glaze over. But as my thoughts dimmed against the new-age, largely white education reformers who didn't live in these neighborhoods and very likely didn't socialize with black or Latino adults in their private life, I started asking, Were they being sent on purpose to destroy poor black and Latino kids? To make sure their minds and emotions and actions were always un-controlled and chaotic, while the schools these white reformers sent *their* kids to were, no doubt, like the thriving and orderly schools I visited in middle- and upper-middle-class neighborhoods? Didn't they see the obvious connection between the behavioral chaos and the low test scores? Why would they make it worse by removing all consequences (and not have genuinely effective therapeutic ones) for outrageous behavior? "Would you send your kids to this school?" I asked one white administrator, a Brown graduate, in a moment of pique. I wasn't asked to sub at that school again.

And what's more, I wasn't the only one to think this or vocal-ize it. I had befriended a black teacher who'd gone to the tough middle school he was now teaching in, and he said to me, "Educa-tion will make you believe in conspiracies, Henderson," and be-moaned how much worse it had gotten. Like that teacher at Cullen I mentioned in the introduction, he'd gone to middle school when there were gang fights between the blacks and Latinos on a regu-lar basis, hardly ideal to be sure, but kids still drew the line at aggression against teachers. One seventh-grader in my friend's class had picked many fights and the administration had not done anything to intervene. It wasn't until the kid assaulted my friend that he was able to get a police protection order simply to have him moved to another class.

Even in the system of "restorative justice"—one of the most popular international alternatives to criminal justice that many tough schools have tried to adopt as a partial replacement for more punitive measures—"offenders" are required to acknowledge the wrong they have done and find the means to repair the damage to the individual they harmed and community they belong to. I sent one kid out of my class after he said "fuck you" to me; he ended up sitting at the principal's desk playing a video game, because, ac-cording to the principal, he needed to "cool off." Another kid said "fuck you" to me at a school I'd been to regularly and then walked out of class. When I spoke to the assistant principal about it he said, "I'm thinking about giving him a detention." He never did. When you tell impulsive and angry kids that no matter what they say to an adult or do to their classmates they will not be sent out of class or sent home, while also not providing other effective means of righting their wrongs, you unleash hell on a school. And if kids couldn't be suspended, detentions didn't work either, because the consequence of skipping detention was always a suspension.

Let me say here, unequivocally, that I do not believe only in the stringent measures—suspensions, expulsions, detentions—that I have mentioned. In fact, I believe deeply in all the soft-power versions of reparative and reformative discipline—meditation, mediation, group therapy, individual therapy, anger management techniques, training in impulse control, and the restorative justice I mentioned above—but they do not work if a school cannot mete out tougher consequences too. The most angry and disruptive kids should not just be tossed onto the street, but they do not belong in schools with the knuckleheads and gems. They have to be given the help, focus, expectations, and consequences they need (we all need) to socialize them into society and into learning. Meditation alone doesn't work on Dick Cheney.

But even the very idea of separating kids out from their peers is being eliminated. Not only are suspensions virtually nonexistent, but, as I mentioned above, principals now ban teachers from even sending a misbehaving child to the principal's office. And the reasons were always baffling: "It takes away their autonomy" or "It takes away from valuable instruction time." But the kid has been stirring up holy hell all period. Is a teacher sending him out really what's impeding instruction?

This rocked me back on my heels and soured my belief in the decency of the people in charge of public schools. When I began subbing, the ban on suspensions was already de facto under way, and no real reason was ever offered up when I asked why. Eventually, years later when the public became aware of it, it would be said that suspensions were inordinately impacting black males and that this racist effect was why they should be banned, but I knew that reason to be a cover story, a straw man hiding something deeper, more complex, and more corrupt, that I couldn't yet figure out. This became the single greatest mystery during my year in public schools. Trying to find the real reason there were no longer consequences for unruly behavior in poor schools (while rich and middle-class schools still had them in place) was the most difficult thing I confronted. It would take me months to unravel it.

In my hunt to figure it out, I first thought that maybe there was something wrong with me. Even though all the veteran black teachers were also horrified by the chaos their schools had descended into, their opinions didn't matter. The new authorities in education (and the education activists who know nothing about the schools they describe) had already identified these teachers as the culprits for their schools' failures, so why should their feelings mean anything? My bewilderment caused me to ask the most basic, commonsense question: Don't all thriving organizations, ecosystems, schools, offices, playgrounds find a way to separate out the 10 to 15 percent of the most "angry, rebellious, disruptive" to keep the whole enterprise from falling apart? If the thriving schools did it, why can't the failing schools?

I suddenly started seeing "separation" everywhere. In 2013, when an LGBT advocate began disrupting a speech Michelle Obama was giving at a Democratic donor's home, the irritated first lady threatened to leave. "One of the things I don't do well is this," she said. "Listen to me or [he] can take the mic, but I'm leaving. You all decide. You have one choice." They chose the first lady and the protester was shown the door. At a gathering held by her husband at the White House, a heckler called out and the president interrupted, "You're in my house." The protester was promptly escorted out to the cheers of Barack Obama's supporters. In early 2018, Obama gave a speech at MIT, the content of which attendees were under strict orders not to leak to the press. They were warned by organizers that if they did so, they would "be subject to removal from the conference and denied tickets to future" events. In a scene from the movie *Inside Out*, a Pixar production that was neurologically and developmentally tested to within an inch of its life, the sullen main character speaks disrespectfully to her parents and her father, taxed from a long day at work, loses his patience and angrily sends her to her room. In the acclaimed film *Moonlight*, about the life of a young gay kid growing up in the projects of Liberty City, Florida, a bully loudly threatens the boy during chemistry class (in a scene that has played out a million times in schools both rich and poor) and the (black) teacher says "Out!" The bully leaves and class resumes.[2]

In April 2015, during a Supreme Court hearing, protesters hiding in the court's audience began shouting their objections to an earlier ruling on campaign finance.[3] These adult protesters were exercising their constitutional right to protest in the midst of the government body whose very job it is to protect that right. Yet they were all shown the door. In Alcoholics Anonymous, you are forbidden to interrupt other participants, and sharing someone else's secrets or identity can get you kicked out.

When I stumbled on the story of "street entrepreneur" Lonnie "Loosie" Warner, I saw separation. Profiled in *The New York Times* in 2011, he'd been arrested more than a dozen times for selling single cigarettes ("loosies") to the denizens of Eighth Avenue who needed a fix but didn't want to cough up the money for a full pack— the same act that got an unarmed Eric Garner killed by a cop in

2014. Warner was widely loved. "There are people who are known bad guys, and then there's [Lonnie]," said a Manhattan district attorney. "He's like the Goodwill Ambassador of Eighth Avenue." Lonnie insisted he provided a valuable service to the denizens of Midtown, but not for the reason you think: according to him, the neighborhood was safer because of what he was doing. Together with his three partners, he kept the truly tough element out. "We don't allow people to sell drugs on this street," Lonnie said. "We just don't allow it." Lonnie knew enough about street life to know that allowing the real drug element in, with its gun violence and brutality, its higher risk and more lucrative reward, would make the block unlivable (and unworkable) for the law-abiding and the minor law–breaking alike. The gems and the knuckleheads could not survive an influx of assholes; they had to be kept or separated out if Eighth Avenue was to continue to thrive. The first two, in the right balance, can live together peaceably, but allow too many of the tough guys to mix in and you're asking for trouble.[4]

But the example of separation that I cared about the most was the story of Elizabeth Spiegel, the chess coach at a low-income middle school in the Bronx. Profiled in Paul Tough's best-selling *How Children Succeed*, she had made the black and brown sixth- and seventh-graders of I.S. 318 into national champions. When one kid, Sebastian, had in her opinion made a boneheaded mistake, she threatened to withdraw him from the tournament if he didn't improve. I recognized that as a type of separation. Another kid, James, was a genius, triumphing over men three times his age in practice tournaments, but he also was a cut-up in school. "In sixth grade he was often sent to the principal's office for goofing around in class." Separation. When James, waiting for his opponent to make his move, wandered away from a game during a tournament to find Spiegel and Tough talking, Spiegel "yelled at him to get back down to the tournament" and that she'd call his father if he didn't. Again, that was a type of separation. I called Spiegel in the course of writing this book and asked her if I.S. 318 had detention. She confirmed that they did.[5]

If every social unit, from one as tiny as a chess club, a family, or a classroom to one as large as a street corner, the Supreme Court, or a political rally, can remove or separate the narrow unruly few—be it a temporary knucklehead like James or permanent ones like the drug dealers on Eighth Avenue—in order to function, why on earth would poor black and Latino schools suddenly be prevented from doing the same? Tough calls this separation "calibrated meanness," but nearly all the tools of calibration (keeping a kid in for recess, sending him to the office, giving him a detention, or suspending him for a day or two for truly egregious unruliness) had vanished from the tough schools I was visiting and it was truly unsettling.

But even before it became clear late in my year of subbing why this was happening, the solution to keeping the schools in tough areas safe and functioning was obvious to me: bring back reform schools. And reform them. Throw the light of day upon them. Make them places of real learning, intellectual, psychological, and emotional, for the 10 to 15 percent who are helpless to subdue their anger. Staff them with the trauma experts and the child psychologists necessary to serve the most deeply troubled youth in whatever measure caring, competent adults are capable of. Model them after schools like Liahona Preparatory Academy in Utah or the Glen Mills Schools in Pennsylvania, the latter of which boast a 65 percent success rate at keeping kids who have had brushes with the law from returning to criminal activity.[6] Offer group therapy and individual therapy; instruct them daily in impulse control and anger management.

Staff them with the thousands of adults who know how to wield firmness and forgiveness, compassion and stringency, the calibrated meanness in the careful, necessary balance all children need to survive. Pay them well to minister to the needs of the neediest among us.

A story on NPR proved to me the miracles that thriving alternative schools can achieve. In 2011, Ryan Speedo Green became one of the few African Americans to win the prestigious Metropolitan National Council Auditions, an opera competition designed to discover and nurture young opera talent. Years before his triumph, however, Green was living a very different life. He was the son of a single mother who struggled with violent moods and did terrible things to him. In fits of rage that spanned much of Green's early years, his mother had knocked him down, kicked him, and attacked him with a closed fist. Green was filled with explosive anger throughout his early life. But in fourth grade he was placed in a class for the most uncontrollable elementary school kids in his Virginia school district (separation!). There he met a teacher named Elizabeth Hughes, a small woman with blond curls, who saw something in him, even at his most angry. Through years of emotional intervention and painful youthful incarceration, he would discover that he had a remarkable singing voice. He would eventually be admitted to a magnet school for the arts in Virginia. The principal was the husband of Ms. Hughes, who had taught him in fourth grade and remembered him from years before. When he finally landed a major part in the opera *La Bohème* at the Met at the age of thirty, Ms. Hughes was in the audience on opening night.

The purpose of stringency, detentions, suspensions, and expulsions along with quality alternative schools for the recalcitrant, the violent, the openly and aggressively defiant, along with therapy and counseling, is to equip them with the emotional and psychological skills they lack, to give them what poor minority students never get in this society: a second, a third, or even a fourth chance after critical mistakes. To train them into the self-mastery they have not come by naturally, while at the same time preventing their anger from activating the combustible knuckleheads and turning a school's entire ecosystem on its head. After a terrifying meltdown, a youthful Green wrote to Ms. Hughes, "I almost need you to be more mean to me." He was grasping for a self-control he did not yet know how to actuate himself and sensed that this adult who loved him could guide him toward it. The purpose of these schools, properly constructed, would be to give troubled students a chance to reveal (to themselves and to the world) that they were perhaps nothing more than knuckleheads in heavy disguise, or reveal, as in the case of Ryan Speedo Green, that they were brilliant, bona fide, marvelously hidden gems all along.

At the beginning of October I was back at Cullen teaching math. I'd been booked there for a three-day assignment. Rodiney was in this class, but his girlfriend, or the girl, I gathered, who had been his girlfriend (the one who told me to "hold up" when I asked her to put her cell phone away), wasn't there, so he was working quietly by himself. His demeanor was frosty, but I didn't mind. He was in that in-between state, neither nice nor rude. He didn't want to act like he liked me, but he didn't want to try me either. When I asked him if he needed help, he just shook his head no. I didn't press. I had a good number of gems in that class that day. I came back a little later to see that Rodiney had gotten a few problems wrong, and I didn't wait to get permission that time. I just jumped in, praised him on the ones he got right, and then focused on correcting his mistakes. "Hey, this is really close, but you didn't bring this variable to the other side of the equation. You almost had it." I moved off and saw him erase his answer and start again. Yeah, at that moment, knucklehead Rodiney was all gem.

There was a knock at the door. It was the football player who'd threatened me with a royal rumble on my first day, standing there with another student. He had been benched by the coach for his grades and his behavior. As he stood at the door, I wasn't sure if he'd gotten the lesson. He saw me and grimaced, as if to say, "Aaah, this dude . . ."

Neither of us were that happy to see each other. I asked him if he had a pass. He fished one out. They don't put names on passes in schools anymore, so I asked him his name.

"C'mon. This my class."

"So what's your name? Your whole name? Middle initial too. 'Cuz I got my roster and I'ma check it."

"You can check. Byron F. Turner."

I loosened up just a bit. He said it with enough confidence that I was inclined to believe him. "What's the F. stand for?"

"Maann, come on."

I turned to the kid with him. "Who are you?"

They looked at each other. Byron shrugged at his buddy, who grinned. This wasn't his buddy's class.

"I'm out," his friend said, giving him a fist bump and hustling off.

Before I let him in I said, "Look, we're not going to have any problems, right?"

"Naw, naw, I'm good," he responded.

He entered and headed to a desk as I handed the work to him, but not before I checked the roster just to be sure. I explained the assignment and told him to let me know if he needed help.

I went back to the teacher's desk. A quick joke between Byron and a friend, and I said, "What did I just say outside, man?" I'd been at this school enough that my reputation as a hard-ass had spread. I wasn't too worried about who had the monopoly of power at that point. And Byron having been chastised by his coach surely helped with that.

"My bad," he said.

He got to work, noticing some of the other students listening to music.

"We can listen to music in here?"

I nodded. "As long as it's on a headset."

"Bet!" He rummaged in his bag and pulled out his phone and got his music going.

After a second I could hear the music through his headphones.

"Turn it down," I said. None of this was said in an especially mean way, but neither was it friendly. I wasn't letting up with him, not at that point. *Do nice things in a mean way.* It's a little mantra I'd come to practice, along with "Don't smile until January," which other teachers had taught me, so kids think you're mean until they find out you're not. He nodded and turned it down.

After a few minutes of what was complete silence, I looked up from the desk. The kids were working diligently. At some point, Rodiney raised his hand for help and I promptly went over to walk him through whatever trouble he was having—a small thaw between us. I was far less sure about Byron. Maybe he rode the line between knucklehead and something worse; maybe if I had let his friend in things would have been different, but right then it didn't matter because he too was working quietly, causing me no stress. There were no assholes in that class, at least not that day. The struggle for the soul of a school is a struggle for the soul of the knuckleheads. And that day, the gems (and the knuckleheads) had won.

4

A Candid World

Why should any of us care deeply whether kids are behaving in school? This is actually a serious philosophical question even if it seems more simplistic than that. After all, it's their future, right? The teachers are there to help them learn, and if students don't want to take advantage of it, that's their business, right? They can choose to throw it all away or not, right? Those questions are, of course, cynical, although I admit that, after a brutal day of dealing with a tough class, I easily and readily told students something along these lines: "This is your life. I have my degree. You can make whatever choice you want right now. It's hurting only you," and then gave up trying to explain some intractable math or science problem to a bunch of kids who were doing anything but listening to me, only to try again once the frustration had passed.

The simple, obvious answer to any questions about the importance of education is that students need an education to be able to earn a living in an increasingly globalized economy. That's not tripe. It's the answer most politicians, Democrat or Republican, will give you. And they are not wrong. But some contemporary political scientists insist that the purpose of public education is something larger, more expansive, than the ability to pay the light bill. They insist the purpose of public schools is to raise children to become active citizens, prepared to engage in the public sphere among enemies, allies, and interlocutors alike. It's called having civic agency and descends from ancient Athens, where Greeks believed men came alive as men only in the public sphere.[1] Today civic agency passes through the doors of U.S. public schools, demanding mighty things of students and teachers alike. As the fundamental business of democracy, civic agency requires a basic competence—the ability to read, write, and listen in the nation's founding tongue. A jury summons, a ballot, and a public debate all require a mind trained in the daily business of democratic language, and it's the job of public schools to train those minds. But if reading competence is necessary for the business of democracy, what of the spirit of democracy? Or, to put it another way, if producing an active citizen is the goal of education, what is the civic goal in asking that a child sit down and shut up while receiving that education?

The mundane answer, of course, is the obvious one, that learning—about rights, responsibilities, or the history of those rights and responsibilities—is impossible if students can't sit still and pay attention. But I believe a separate, larger goal of learning to behave is also at play in schools and that it can be traced directly to the most important document of our nation's founding, the Declaration of Independence. Its opening is familiar enough: "When in the Course of human Events, it becomes necessary for one People to dissolve the Political Bands which have connected them with another, and to assume among the Powers of the Earth, the separate and equal Station to which the Laws of Nature and of Nature's God entitle them, a decent Respect to the Opinions of Mankind requires that they should declare the causes which impel them to the Separation." The Declaration then goes on to enumerate the self-evident truths, followed by pointed reference to the "long Train of Abuses and Usurpations" that reveal a "Design to reduce" those truths "under absolute Despotism," and concludes, "Such has been the patient sufferance of these Colonies. To prove this, let Facts be submitted to a candid world."

"A decent respect." "Patient sufferance." "Submitted." And elsewhere the Declaration of Independence declares the virtue of prudence and makes its overall case in "the most humble terms," as it outlines for the world to see the colonists' many grievances against the British king. And, more crucially, for the world to approve. In other words, about 250 years ago the progenitors of what would become the world's oldest and most successful democracy were practicing what in some quarters is known today as respectability politics.[2] When teachers insist on the importance of proper behavior for young people, poor and otherwise, when they insist that students learn how to subdue their bodies and minds, the powerful civic goal is not to prepare them for a job in the global economy but to prepare them for a fight.[3]

Piqued by the angry and largely racist objections of whites (and the more sympathetic quarrel of an older generation of blacks) to the Black Lives Matter movement, the critics Ta-Nehisi Coates and Roland Martin have written derisively of the idea that behavior is important. Implicitly critiquing the controlled and respectful nonviolent protests of the 1960s, Coates and Martin insist that only black people are asked to be humble in their protests, respectable in their objections, prudent and deferential in asking for overdue reforms and God-given rights. They rightly ask: Why do politeness and a spotless record matter when unarmed black men are being senselessly slaughtered? This is a righteous question, and a righteous cause animates it. And black dignity surely has a right to its rage. But Coates et al. are wrong. Respectability politics is not something condescendingly assigned to blacks or specific to this age. It descends on every actor seeking allies in contests of rights and freedoms. The early colonists knew that the king had allies, monarchs across the globe who had their own restless populations and would be loath to do anything that might stoke rebellion among them. The founders, despite their anger at being menaced by the king, nevertheless needed allies—they needed strangers to trust them—so they proceeded with prudence and humility in laying out their grievances against the king. But respectability is even older than that. In ancient Athens, the birthplace of Western-style democracy, a citizen had to be a citizen in good standing or face *atimia*, meaning a total deprivation of rights. If a citizen had not paid his debts or had been cruel to his parents, he would be barred from participating in the business of the polis. He lacked standing, respectability, in the eyes of his fellow citizens and could in fact be killed by a citizen, who would not be considered to have committed a crime.

Today is no different. When a famous conservative legal scholar chastises the courts for responding to what he sees as Donald Trump's "norm-busting . . . [attacks] on institutions" with "norm-breaking behavior of their own" and insists that courts "bend over backwards to be circumspect to maintain the informal norms that inform [their] legitimacy," he is counseling a version of respectability politics in the face of what he sees as the executive branch's wholesale lack of respectability.[4] When the president of the University of Virginia warned counter-demonstrators not to confront the marchers of the Unite the Right movement who planned to descend on Charlottesville in protest of the removal of Confederate statues, writing, "I urge students and all UVA community members to avoid the August 12 rally and avoid physical confrontation generally . . . to approach the rally and confront the activists would only satisfy their craving for spectacle. They . . . really *want* confrontation; do not gratify their desire," she was counseling a version of respectability politics.[5] Neither commentator was aiming warnings at blacks alone.

The long-ago colonists needed strangers to be their friend—the consent of the candid world—if they were to stand a chance against a mighty government power. And as political theorist Danielle Allen has pointed out, in volatile democracies (then and now), strangers feel encouraged to trust you when they feel your cause is righteous, when its proponents proceed with prudence, humility, and a decent respect for the opinions of humanity.

In contemporary times this remains a dispiriting concept for disadvantaged minorities to hear: that we need other people's approval to pursue our fight for freedom. It feels like an extension of oppression to be told that we must behave properly so the majority will like us enough to join our fight. Part of independence, surely, means not bending to please anyone, friend or foe. And the elixir of prideful, unaided independence has always been a powerful one. A dramatic recent example that set Black Twitter on fire came in early 2016. The TV actor Jesse Williams, who appears on the show *Grey's Anatomy*, received a BET Award for his political activism. He gave a stirring speech about the Black Lives Matter movement, speaking on behalf of the "activists, the civil rights attorneys, the struggling parents, the teachers, the students that are realizing that a system . . . built to divide . . . and destroy us cannot stand if we do." I sat bolt upright listening to that, moved from the outset. He pressed on powerfully through as sharp a condemnation of police brutality and political indifference as the modern civil rights movement had yet seen. Then, in the middle of the speech, he landed here: "So what's gonna happen is we're going to have equal rights and justice in our country, or we will restructure their function, and ours."[6] He got a standing ovation halfway through his speech. He was invited to appear on *Ellen* and brought to the White House by Barack Obama. I cheered from my living room and followed him on Twitter.

But even as I cheered him (even retyping it now I feel a surge of excitement), I knew this was not real. It was a fantasy as old as the first black people who arrived in the New World's dream of a return home to Africa. There is no "restructuring their function and ours," no brand-new all-black nation to be built, certainly not from scratch, not on this soil; this country is who and where we are. To those of us living, in no small measure, as native exiles within this nation's borders, it is truly enchanting to believe that we can break off and go it alone, but the fight against that exile can be waged here and only here. And training young people to join it is no small part of the business of education.

So what does it mean to properly train a child for a fight? First, it acknowledges that all of us rely on "democratic strangers" for help. The largest political parties are bands of strangers. Before the rise of Trump, the Democratic party consisted of blacks, working-class whites, and progressive liberals; Republicans were largely Christian conservatives, millionaire bankers, and libertarians. Though the groups within each party spent next to no time in each other's actual company (they were strangers), they showed up faithfully every four years to pull the lever for their own team; they felt safer in each other's imagined company than anyone else's.

Second, it acknowledges the fragile, perhaps dispiriting, fact that we are all more likely to trust a stranger who behaves respectably. When lawyers manage to keep a defendant's past misdeeds from being introduced into evidence, they are working a respectability angle. When prosecutors introduce proof of how loving and charitable the victim was, they are working a respectability angle. When the morally and psychically wounded ached enough at the killings of unarmed black men to start a hashtag that blossomed into Black Lives Matter, it was because the men were *unarmed*. That is, they were behaving respectably, yet they were still murdered. Had the men been waving guns, threatening cops, there would be no movement, only bewildered distress.

And finally, preparing a child for a fight means being aware of the unique and mortally unfair perils that disadvantaged children face in this country. And that exempting them from prudence and respectability out of inordinate pride only dooms them to fight a war alone.

The best example of a child who embodied these ideals was a six-year-old named Ruby Bridges. She was a marvel, born the same year the U.S. Supreme Court ruled in *Brown v. Board of Education* (1954) that schools must be desegregated. In an effort to remain segregated, New Orleans devised a test to determine which black children would be selected to integrate white schools and made the test as difficult as possible. In 1960 the NAACP told Ruby's parents that she was one of only six African American children to pass the test and that she would be the first child to integrate an all-white elementary school in the South. To do so she ran a frightening gauntlet with otherworldly calm, escorted to school by the federal marshals requested by a U.S. District Court judge.[7] A children's book about her life, *The Story of Ruby Bridges*, describes how Ruby walked to school escorted by U.S. marshals for months as crowds of white people screamed at her and called her vicious names. The whites in the area had refused to send their children to school with Ruby, so she sat alone in her class each day with just her teacher, Ms. Henry. Despite having no one to play or learn or eat lunch with, Ruby went to class happy and excited to learn. Ruby, according to Ms. Henry, "was polite and she worked well at her desk. She didn't seem nervous or anxious or irritable or scared. She seemed as normal and relaxed as any child I've ever taught. . . . Sometimes I'd look at her and wonder how she did it."[8]

Then one day, according to the book, after months of enduring the rage and aggression, Ruby suddenly stopped in the middle of the protesters and stared back at them and seemed to speak for a few minutes. She then quickly turned back and hurried on to school. Ms. Henry had watched from the window and asked Ruby why she had suddenly stopped to talk to the angry crowd.

"I didn't stop and talk with them," she said.

"Ruby, I saw you talking," Ms. Henry says. "I saw your lips moving."

' "I wasn't talking," said Ruby. "I was praying. I was praying for them."

This is a story not easily repeated in this or any age. And however Ruby Bridges developed that preternatural poise and self-control, it prepared her to walk straight into the mouth of a raging storm. She had, at a tender age, mastery of her body and mind. She would not be provoked to wrath.

The vast majority of young people will never be called on in this way, but it doesn't matter. The process of emotional regulation that allowed a young child like Ruby to march unprovoked into the newly desegregated Louisiana school in the face of hostile strangers is dictated and controlled by the same physiological system that children in classrooms must use every day to regulate their emotions when being picked on in class, getting a bad grade in math, or being chastised by an adult. It was first forged during our earliest days on the planet and is built into all of us. All children must learn to regulate that system—be they the middle-class children of Summerhill or the underserved youth of inner-city Los Angeles. William Blake's famous poem "Infant Sorrow" points to the volatile well of emotions with which each child is born:

My mother groaned! my father wept
Into the dangerous world I leapt:
Helpless, naked, piping loud,
Like a fiend hid in a cloud.

Struggling in my father's hands,
Striving against my swaddling bands,

Bound and weary, I thought best
To sulk upon my mother's breast.

Each child must be taught to bind the fiend inside them. But the most popular new ideas in education have shown that this may be especially difficult for schools educating poor kids, not least because the authority figures (the groaning mother, the weeping father) are struggling too. The most recent research suggests that children who experience early trauma—the type endemic to poor, single-parent communities, especially those riven by drugs, crime, parental absenteeism, and environmental hazards—find it especially difficult to manage the stressors of daily life. And as a result of this difficulty, they have a tougher time concentrating, dealing with boredom, or regulating their temper. But this is why it is even more important that students from disadvantaged backgrounds be taught in environments that insist on self-mastery. And that they be provided both sympathy and commonsense stringency to guide them toward it.

While this may seem to have been confined to the inner cities of the United States, it won't be forever. A recent article in *The Wall Street Journal*, "The Children of the Opioid Crisis," has made plain that it will happen in the heartland too.[9] The terror these children face will spill into their schools soon enough. We should, thus, be training children in impulse control from the earliest of ages in every school, in every town, and every city, from Huntsville, Alabama, to Harlem and other tough neighborhoods in New York City. It is an easy and necessary fix for troubled schools and troubled kids.

Because of what I saw so plainly in these poor schools, I became curious about the details of how successful schools, be they middle- and upper-middle-class or disadvantaged ones, were operating. How were thriving schools dealing with impulsive behavior? I'd heard no cursing from the high schoolers at LA High, although I'm sure they cursed outside adult earshot all the time, but what of other schools? If self-regulation and civic agency are more pressing for the black and the poor, who still live in this country under the "inescapable social accusation of race," as critic Helen Vendler has described it, what do stringency, boundaries, and the tools of self-moderation and self-control look like in well-run middle- and upper-middle-class schools?[10] I went into the school district's database and expanded my sub area. I wanted, in essence, to see how the other half lived.

From doing this, I became convinced that, along with encouragement and laughter, and a deep and abiding love for kids, stringency (consequences for actions) was *always* in place when a school was thriving but no discernable discipline was visible at schools that were failing. At the Los Angeles Center for Enriched Studies in West LA, the crown jewel of Los Angeles public schools, the largest document on the teacher's desk was a carbon-layered detention form. Detention was held once a week, and students who missed it had to show up for Saturday detention. Recall, by contrast, the middle school where several teachers had quit after being assaulted by students, a kid had crack on him, and the teachers laughed about still trying to even *establish* a discipline system.

In other words, the myth of Summerhill was exactly that—a myth, even in the poor schools that were thriving. I began to see stringency everywhere. An article in the *Los Angeles Times*, "No Gold Stars for Excellent LA Teaching: Effective Instructors Get Little Recognition," profiled third-grade teacher Zenaida Tan, who was teaching her students in a low-income LA school how to multiply 7,850,437,826 by 56. For years she had brought kids who were below grade level up to advanced-level math over the course of a year. The article was aimed at trying to unravel the secret to her and other talented teachers' success, but never managed to pinpoint any one trait. Hard work, love, innovative ideas, and high expectations were all different suggestions. But what resonated with me in that three-thousand-plus-word article was this: Tan "says her fellow teachers consider her strict, even mean." An adult who'd been Tan's student twenty years earlier recalled, "I really didn't like her [as a kid]. I remember crying every day. Now I recognize it wasn't mean, it was strict. She was pushing me to do what I was capable of. . . . I don't think I'll ever forget her."

Another teacher profiled in the same article taught Shakespeare. And all I could see was the stringent part of what she said: "If the teacher's expectations are high, *and you have control of the classroom*, those kids should do well."[11] Now recall the huge number the "mean" Tan was getting her third-graders to multiply ($7{,}850{,}437{,}826 \times 56$) and compare it to the week I spent in an out-of-control sixth-grade math class in a charter school: there was no detention, no suspension, and no parent answered the phone when I called their homes; kids were literally climbing in and out of the windows and I went hoarse yelling at them to stop misbehaving; when I asked kids to write out 5 million as a number, out of a class of nineteen kids only three of them got it right, one kid having written 500.

An article in *The Atlantic*, "What Makes a Great Teacher?," attempted to do the same thing the *LA Times* article did, insisting on a lot of high-minded reasons successful teachers thrive: "First, great teachers tended to set big goals. They were also perpetually looking for ways to improve their effectiveness . . . they maintained focus . . . they planned exhaustively; and they worked relentlessly." I agreed with all of that. But in a profile of a teacher named William Taylor, I also saw stringency.

> On a typical Monday, Mr. Taylor's kids come to class and begin silently working on the Problem of the Day written on the blackboard. [Silent fifth-graders? That's unusual.] . . . Mr. Taylor walks in and says good morning. "Good morning!" they answer in kid

unison. [Again unusual. Elementary students don't naturally answer in unison. Nor are they working quietly in a teacher's absence.]

The lesson begins and Mr. Taylor cycles through a few activities,
with the problems getting harder each time. The kids who get it
right, and many do, "whisper-shout 'Yes!'" Why whisper? I wondered. Then there's this:

> "Now I'm going to trick you," Mr. Taylor says. "What's 3 times
> 120?" The orange cards [on which kids write their answers] go
> down and back up. "Ooh, ooh, ooh!" says one little girl, unable
> to contain herself. "'Ooh'? Is that the answer?" Mr. Taylor says,
> silencing her.[12]

And there it was, again! The writer made no mention of it, but what
I saw was a person who while teaching his students math was also
training them in impulse control. Yes, he was brilliant and inven-
tive, but he was also stringent. What parent wouldn't want Taylor
teaching their child math?

Because the reporter was looking for one thing, she found it.
The takeaway was supposed to be that teachers just have to work
on their fun ideas, never get any sleep, work their fingers to the
bone, and kids will naturally answer in unison, naturally stay quiet
in class, naturally keep their hands to themselves, naturally behave.
The better the quality of your lesson plans, the better behaved kids
will be. But that's just nonsense. Kids also need stringency to learn
to contain themselves, even if the lesson is nothing more than
Taylor's rejoinder: "'Ooh'? Is that the answer?"

Even Paul Tough, the writer of the most celebrated book in
contemporary education, after exploring the many psychological
traumas that led children to misbehave and fall behind in school,
concluded of his, and every parent's, role in the raising of his own

son that as he "grew older . . . I found, as countless parents had found before me, that he needed something more than love and hugs. He also needed discipline, rules, limits; someone to say no." But no one was saying no to these kids in the toughest schools. They had license to do as they pleased, and all I could ask myself, what felt like a conspiracy theory, was what were they preparing poor black and Latino students for: to be like Ruby Bridges, or to become easy fodder for violent cops?

In his concept of education, A. S. Neill believed that self-government "would never succeed unless the teacher believes that all authority is dangerous for the child." He wanted a world in which "no boy would learn to read a word until he desired to read; no boy would do anything unless he wanted to do it." And that above all else, "the first thing a child should learn to be is a rebel."[13] Neill is exactly wrong. A child must first be made to bend before he can properly rebel. Before she can turn into an adult who will make the world bend, she must first learn to listen and get others to listen. And even then, she will need allies, democratic strangers, to trust her enough to let her lead them.

After Jesse Williams, perhaps the most spectacular moment of racial protest came in the summer of 2016 when Colin Kaepernick, the professional football player, became outraged by the slaughter of unarmed black men and found his fumbling way to respectability politics. Today all of us who are horrified by these killings openly regard him as a hero and rightly so. But to watch him in the early fall of 2016, as he sat defiantly during the national anthem, his afro floating atop his head like an architect's dome, was to watch a young man struggling to find a voice. The press was relentless. During a practice session a day or two later, he wore socks that sported the image of pigs dressed as cops. He won few friends. He was fighting the wrong fight or fighting the right fight the wrong way. Some people, potential allies, rebuked him. Most vociferous was Khalilah Camacho Ali, an ex-wife of Muhammad Ali, who suggested a more humble approach. In the interim the nation watched as Kaepernick heeded the advice of a former Green Beret who had written to Kaepernick to say that though he acknowledged his right to protest, he felt jarred by the sight of seeing the quarterback sitting during the anthem and the raising of the flag. They came to a meeting of the minds.[14]

Kaepernick had the humility to listen to what the army veteran had to say. Soon the pig socks and the afro were gone. Kaepernick tied his hair back and chose instead to kneel during "The Star-Spangled Banner." In the press room afterward, he spoke clearly and passionately about his push for justice and vowed he would continue to kneel. And the candid world convulsed again but differently this time. The haters were still vocal; even his white parents expressed outrage. But there was something else too. The simple and humble act of kneeling during the anthem stirred something in many who were watching, precisely because of how respectful it was. The kneeling position is the timeless pose of humility. Knights kneel before kings. Kings kneel before popes. Men kneel before the woman they ask to marry. The act implies dignity and obligation, modesty and strength all at once. Jay-Z glosses his line about knighthood in "Most Kings" as "someone kneeling . . . to accept the honor of being knighted." The MSNBC host Joy-Ann Reid wrote in defense of Kaepernick on Twitter, "Kneeling is a sign of supplication to God. It's done in church every Sunday. It's a symbol of prayer."[15] And what Pee Wee football player hasn't heard their coach say "Take a knee"?

Other football players raised their fists during the anthem. One team locked arms, one or two others sat defiantly during the anthem, but only the knee found true allies. Shortly after Kaepernick knelt, other players in the National Football League did too. Then so did an entire football team in Oregon that had black and white players. In the first-round playoffs of the Women's National Basketball Association in 2016, the entire Indiana Fever team knelt. So did the entire band of a black college and a retired white veteran who was a spectator at a volleyball game in Texas. By the time the season ended and a new season started, the silent protests had electrified the nation. Black cops in New York spoke out in defense of Kaepernick. White football players joined their black comrades in kneeling at the start of the season. A Major League Baseball player knelt. Derek Jeter, a new owner of the Miami Marlins, said any player on his team was welcome to exercise his freedom of speech. The image of the kneeling player became the iconic image of modern racial protest. A Twitter account eventually proclaimed, "My 80 percent white hometown in Arkansas is displaying a black lives matter flag."[16]

And as his humble example took hold, Kaepernick found himself on the cover of *Time* magazine, selected as *GQ*'s man of the year, and receiving the Sports Illustrated Legacy Award, hailed as the second coming of Muhammad Ali.[17] Kaepernick, and his countless allies, naturally found powerful enemies, to be sure, the current president chief among them. But Kaepernick remains undeterred, sensing the gravity of his example. Speaking on the death threats he'd received, Kaepernick remained defiant: "If [I am killed], you've proved my point and it will be loud and clear for everyone why it happened."[18] Today no team in the NFL will hire him, and according to polls he is despised by a large swath of football fans, even more than players who have murdered or raped people. But humility does not guarantee freedom from enemies (Martin Luther King Jr., a man who loved peace, was assassinated); it simply helps you find allies in the fight against those enemies.

In a deeply felt thread a white Twitter user lashed out at the treatment of Kaepernick:

> Really struck by the fact that Kaepernick's ongoing silent, peaceful protest was deeply, rage-inducingly unacceptable to white America.

I mean, it was *literally* an example of everything that Black America is told that protest *must* be to be acceptable. But it wasn't.

Didn't damage property. Didn't block traffic. Didn't interrupt shopping. Didn't make noise. Didn't even say anything, until someone asked.

And now, they cheer that Kaepernick is out of work. As he literally donates his earnings to feed people whose meals they're defunding.

I don't put much weight behind "breaking rules will hurt the cause," in large part because i watch what happens when people DO follow them. Kaepernick's treatment is a prime example of what PoC mean when they critique "respectability politics."

Someone responded to his thread by writing, "Are you surprised?" His response:

Not surprised, just struck by the simple clarity of this particular example.[19]

To me this was exactly, thrillingly, wrong. And I tweeted as much. It was precisely Kaepernick's humility that bound this tweeter to him, that made him see the glaring moral bankruptcy of Kaepernick's enemies. The "simple clarity" of Kaepernick's example pointed straight to the moral corruption of the people who reviled him. The tweeter was convinced of the righteousness of Kaepernick's cause because of the righteousness of Kaepernick's example.

Courage does not always require reason. A philosopher (I forget which one) tells the story of a man who risks his life in an instant to grab hold of a child to whom he is not related but sees crawling toward a cliff. Instinct, some natural spur to altruism, mobilized him without a thought to what he was doing. But sustained courage, the kind that brings about political change in a democracy, does take reason and patience and the ability to subdue the egotistical self. Kaepernick, like Ruby Bridges before him, had learned somehow to subdue his own mind and body, to swallow the trepidation that inheres in taking a dangerous stand, to heed a wise mentor's advice, to remain steadfast against his own parents' rebuke, to face even the real threat of death, and press on.

Children who cannot subdue their own bodies and minds can never find their way toward the type of freedom all children need. And in the hands of wise educators the purpose of stringency, not just sweetness, is to slowly train children toward that self-control. When we do otherwise we are not giving them freedom. We are giving them license. Who knows where the next great leader of black American life will come from? We can no more guarantee the emergence of a moral genius than we can an artistic one. But they do emerge, they do come. And the lasting moral heroes almost never come from the man who was violent and volatile, wholly unsubdued, as a child. A writer, chastising young chefs fascinated by the latest and glitziest methods of cooking while eschewing the rudimentary lessons taught by Auguste Escoffier, the great modernizer of French cuisine, insisted that young chefs must be subdued by Escoffier before they could successfully resist him. This is what a judge meant when he said to a famous philosopher, "The only men who have freedom of choice in matters of religion as adults were those who were indoctrinated in religion as a child." This is what the literary critic Helen Vendler meant when she wrote that "criticism is the revenge of the student who once, perforce, sat silent while things that seemed untrue were said unrebuked."[20]

Martin Luther dutifully absorbed the teachings of the Catholic Church before rebelling against the teachings of the Catholic Church. But without the absorption, perforce, the sitting silent, he would not have had the intellectual capacity, the patience, the controlled vengeance to rebuke the things that were untrue. This is what Gustave Flaubert, inventor of the modern novel, meant when he said, "Be regular and ordinary in your life . . . so that you may be violent and original in your work." The practiced nonviolence of Martin Luther King Jr. and the movement he led inflicted more original violence on the Old South than at any time since the Civil War. The measure of how dangerous his subdued respectability was? He paid for it with his life. History's hero is the student whose angry patience ties her to the mast of unjust rules she will one day overturn. The angry and rebellious student of today will become history's defeated.

I want to close this section with one last tweetstorm about Black Lives Matter. When it first burst into the national consciousness, the protest group was roundly criticized for its tactics by ill-intended whites and well-intended blacks. Critics pointed to the movement's disruptiveness: its members' tendency to run en masse into the middle of traffic with protest signs; their commandeering of the mic at election rallies, angrily confronting Hillary Clinton, the only candidate who gave them time, for her failures. These were by no means their only tactics but they were the ones that got the most press and helped their enemies demonize the movement's laudable desire to bring attention to the urgent crisis of police killings. The deliberate lack of organized hierarchy, elected leaders, or official representatives, however, largely meant anyone could do something in the name of Black Lives Matter, and the organization had no formal means of expulsion or chastisement. (We forget that Martin Luther King Jr. was the *elected* head of the Southern Christian Leadership Conference and was thus answerable to the membership.) But after violence erupted in Charlottesville, Virginia, in 2017, as armed neo-Nazis and other white supremacists descended on the college town to protest the removal of a Confederate statue, Black Lives Matter was implicated but differently this time. At a rally of the same forces in Boston, shortly after the one in Virginia, a white eyewitness reported this:

> Y'all should hear about my experience with BLM at the Boston Anti-Nazi Rally.
>
> I want that to be crystal clear. BLM marshals were *preventing* fights from breaking out.
>
> At one point they were escorting a Nazi out of the rally near where I was standing.
>
> Nazi dropped his flag. I snatched for it. He picked it up. I yanked at it.
>
> The BLM marshal next to me whupped the back of my head. [And shouted] "DON'T!"
>
> At that moment he stopped me from possibly sparking a riot.
>
> I was stupid. I was ready to escalate. BLM *stopped* me.
>
> This is no surprise to anyone who has actually been to a BLM event or worked with them.[21]

At least these members of Black Lives Matter somehow made their way toward respectability by stringently demanding peace and self-control even in the face of violent emotions, protecting hate-filled enemies against the aggression of titular allies. The practiced self-control required of a black person to escort Nazis to safety is hard to imagine.

When we release poor students (or any students) from the obligation to subdue their own immediate instincts, we are preparing them for a life of failure and chaos. If they're black, we're preparing them for the total triumph of an armed enemy who would stalk a kid through the streets of his own Florida hometown, shoot and kill him, and then declare self-defense when that frightened kid fought for his life. Though Trayvon Martin's killer has gone unpunished, Martin's death sparked outrage and helped fuel a movement because he'd done nothing wrong but attempt to be free. Respectability increases, even in small measure, the chance to have allies in a noble fight, the chance to secure the help of strangers, when, after long nights of suffering, a beleaguered people declare their grievances before a candid world.

5

Stamped from the Beginning

I have so far confined my comments to life inside schools attended by poor black and Latino students and how to improve those schools, but I am generally interested in black students as a whole and in understanding how they navigate the world. For this reason, naturally, black kids in predominantly white schools and how they are faring is also of interest to me. The few times I was assigned to such schools in LA, I always enjoyed the few black students and they seemed to always enjoy me. After my first day of subbing at Fairfax High in a class that, coincidentally, was mostly black, though the school was anything but, the teacher called me whenever she had to be absent. I was always happy to see the students there.

But another aspect of that school, something I didn't yet understand, were the reports on suspensions. Even in my second month of subbing, as I indicated in chapter 3, I did not understand why all the disciplinary measures of a generation ago, the calibrated meanness—detention, suspension, even just sending kids to the principal's office—had vanished. The rumors of zero tolerance, of which I was also only dimly aware, were just rumors. Many schools seemed to tolerate just about anything. I understood well enough that detention had vanished because suspension was the natural punishment for missing detention; no one would go to detention if skipping it had no consequences.

Beginning to percolate in education circles (or the professional development seminars I had to attend), even before stories began to hit the press, was that one reason for doing away with suspensions was that black students, especially boys, were getting suspended from white schools at a higher rate than the white kids. When the disparity finally did make national news, many school leaders seized on it as an opportunity to announce a ban on suspensions. The implication, I think, was that racist white schools were punishing black boys for infractions for which white boys were not punished and that only a full moratorium on suspensions could put an end to the unfairness. I became convinced that racism was involved, even if it wasn't obvious. But I also knew the statistics were hiding the real reason; I just didn't know what that reason was. I had already taught in many poor black charter and traditional public schools that had done away with suspensions de facto, but I was still confounded as to why. It gnawed at me, but I let my frustration and exhaustion simmer.

I did, however, become keener to understand the life of black kids, especially boys, in predominantly white schools. I wasn't sure that they all were behaving like angels and being unfairly maligned, but I knew that it was a definite possibility. I kept thinking about what a friend once said to me: "Being a black man is an exact science and they want us all to fail." My experience of "integrated schools" (you'll understand the quotation marks shortly) was perhaps the most unsettling and most confounding experience I had during the year I spent teaching. It was a riddle inside an already vexing set of riddles, and mapping it to its source meant arriving at the single most improbable, accidental, perhaps even comical source of a host of bizarre and disquieting racial problems. That source's name was Mariah Carey. Bear with me and I'll explain.

In 1990 Carey released her first studio album. It sold nine million copies. Many hailed her as the second coming of Whitney Houston, the then-reigning diva of American popular music. Carey's handlers, led by her husband, the Sony Music impresario Tommy Mottola, carved out her niche with Houston as her foil, subtly pressing the notion that whatever Houston could do, Carey could do better. Sure, Houston had pipes, but she inherited them from her gospel-singing mother; Carey's were sui generis (never mind that her mother was an opera singer). Houston had a three-octave range; Carey had a five-octave range. Houston was just a voice; Carey, a singer *and* songwriter, had a brain. But the main difference in our thoroughly racialized world never needed to be spoken: Mariah Carey was white; Whitney Houston was black. Today we forget that thirty years ago Carey, straight of hair and white of skin, was introduced to the world without any acknowledgment that she had one parent with a possibly mixed racial heritage. A few discerning eyes in the black community may have wondered whether Carey had a "drop" of black blood in her, but no hint was made of Mariah's mixed ancestry until well after she was dominating the airwaves and had swept the awards season the year her first album was released. The tension between the two megawatt stars was real. I worked behind the scenes at the 1999 Oscars when Houston was overheard saying of Carey, with whom she was to sing their middling hit "When You Believe," "She can't go where I wanna go. She can't sing what I wanna sing."

Although no one of any musical intelligence would seriously dispute Houston's superior vocal gift, Carey's impact on the next generation of popular singers, black and white, surpassed that of any of the singers before her. And, as one music critic noted, once Carey began to speak a bit more openly about her father's mixed heritage and make more black-sounding music, she, "more than any other musician, established R&B and hip-hop as the sound of pop."[1] But it wasn't just the sound; it was the face too. Carey inaugurated a dramatic and unsettling change in America's race relations, a contemporary cultural version of Jim Crow that now dominates American culture. And it shows up in integrated schools in alarming ways.

New York Times Magazine reporter Nikole Hannah-Jones won a National Magazine Award in 2017 for the account of her search for a quality, integrated school for her daughter in New York. In it she argued for a renewed social commitment to integration as the only reasonable path forward for black students, otherwise locked in substandard local schools in segregated neighborhoods. The article tracked the successful life stories of Hannah-Jones and her husband, both of whom attended integrated schools as kids. The gross economic disparities black kids face could, she argued, be permanently ameliorated only by sending black kids to schools with the types of middle-class, politically connected white families that abound in pockets of New York. The essay solidified Hannah-Jones's much-deserved reputation as an insightful and original voice on modern race relations. But my experience of teaching in "integrated environments," including, in one instance, a private school, was vastly different from Hannah-Jones's integrated school experience and suggests real and rarely remarked-on perils for black students today, some of which Hannah-Jones and her husband were shielded from a generation ago, when openly declared racism was in some ways a far more volatile component of black life.

One of those perils is hidden inside the very meaning of the word *integration*. Truly integrated schools are almost impossible in the United States, not feasible for the majority of black kids. With the exception of a handful of major cities like New York, where several ethnic groups are sizably represented, integration more often means a school where the vast majority of white kids is sprinkled with a light dusting of black and brown ones.* Blacks, after all, constitute 11 percent of the U.S. population, whereas whites still account for upward of 60 percent, or as high as 70 percent if you count whites who speak Spanish.

Hannah-Jones's own experience growing up in segregated Idaho reflects this. Her parents, a working-class couple, sent her to an affluent white public school where she was one of the few black students. It changed the trajectory of her life. "My parents chose one of the whitest, richest schools, thinking it would provide the best opportunities for us," she writes. "I was among the tiny number of working-class children and the even tinier number of black children. . . . We showed up in a yellow bus, visitors in someone else's neighborhood, and were whisked back across the bridge each day as soon as the bell rang." And though the experience was challenging, Hannah-Jones is nevertheless grateful for it: "I remember those years as emotionally and socially fraught, but also as academically stimulating and world-expanding. Aside from the rigorous classes and quality instruction I received, this exposure helped me imagine possibilities, a course for myself that I had not considered before." Hannah-Jones goes on to attribute her greatest achievement to her integrated schooling: "I have no doubt my parents' decision to pull me out of my segregated neighborhood school made the possibility of my getting from there to here—staff writer for *The New York Times Magazine*—more likely."[2]

My own family had a story similar to hers, though the results were different. When my father died, my mother, anxious about what would become of my younger brother, who no longer had a father at home and whose older siblings were away at college, re-

---

* The reverse is also the case, heavy on the brown and black with a dusting of white, which is not the integration Hannah-Jones believes to be of political and economic benefit to the brown and black kids, but was ultimately the type of school she sent her daughter to.

moved him from our local public schools when he was fourteen and placed him in a white private school. She spent the tiny pension my father had left her on my brother's tuition and took out loans to afford the rest. I quote at length what he wrote me of his experience:

> I would like to start off by saying that my high school [years] were some of the most memorable as well as enjoyable of my lifetime. Spending a few years with roughly the same 60 to 70 people, who were mostly all from upper-middle-class families, allows you certain privileges that you wouldn't ordinarily have. Nor would your peers who don't go to schools like these.
>
> But when I first started going to Hudson [at age fourteen], I gave them their nigger. I don't know why I did this; I came out of the public school system and there I was the nerd. But when I went to Hudson, I was always picking fights that I never escalated. I don't know why I did that. I played this tough-guy act up through the eighth grade. It must have subsided quite a bit by the time I was in the tenth grade, because by then I had decided to be more myself. Meaning that I went from the thug type to the Oreo type, then to the black type. It's weird. (I can explain more on the phone.)[3]

This describes a very different experience, and journey, than Hannah-Jones's. The youthful Hannah-Jones had a great unaccounted for advantage over my brother that helped her thrive in her "integrated" world: she wasn't a boy. A 2013 study of school-age children in England found that young boys in schools where they are economically disadvantaged relative to their peers fare far worse behaviorally than similarly disadvantaged girls. *The Economist* reported: "Researchers . . . followed over 1,600 children from age five to age 12 in England and Wales . . . [They] found that poor boys living in largely well-to-do neighbourhoods were the most likely to engage in anti-social behaviour, from lying and swearing to such petty misdemeanours as fighting, shoplifting and vandalism. [In contrast] poor boys in the poorest neighbourhoods were the least likely to run into trouble."[4] A study of boys in the United States backed up these findings. A researcher found that boys who lived in poor neighborhoods surrounded by more affluent ones were more likely to get into trouble than boys who lived in areas that were uniformly poor. Poor boys, surrounded by affluence, had more drug-using friends, more anxiety and psychological distress than boys who lived in areas where the economic conditions were uniform. These results did not hold true for girls, who "had fewer delinquent friends and believed more in their ability to attend college and get a good job."[5]

But what about Hannah-Jones's husband, whose integrated schooling she credits for his success? Why was he able to thrive in his presumably wealthier, integrated school but my brother and the boys from these studies didn't? Because, I suspect, her husband's education was qualitatively different from hers. His classmates weren't wealthier. He grew up an army brat and went to schools in Europe with the sons and daughters of other army officers, during a time when the army was more than 25 percent black; also, the pay his parents received, as government employees, was the same as that of any white enlisted officer. Her husband did not experience the economic disparities that Hannah-Jones experienced as a child. (I had confirmation of this hunch when I met a black Uber driver whose parents were army officers and had raised him in Germany. He was working for Uber to pay his way through college for an electrical engineering degree. He'd gone to Heidelberg High School, in Heidelberg, Germany, where, according to him, the school was split evenly between black and white students. He said there were never any problems between the black and white kids and that he loved growing up there. In other words, Hannah-Jones's husband's and this driver's integrated environment was, unlike my brother's or Hannah-Jones's, an example of true racial and economic integration and so both he and Hannah-Jones's husband were able to flourish without any feelings of inadequacy about their station in life relative to richer boys.)

The studies I cited above bear out what my brother reported—that he was keenly aware of the wealth of the white students around him—and the experience of a black student I got to know at a private school where I taught briefly. He had been adopted from Africa as a child by a white family but was the only fully black kid at the school of several hundred and had two white sisters; the handful of other black kids were biracial. The adopted boy was in middle school (the age when emotional difficulties become most pronounced) and had continually found himself in trouble. I felt terrible for him. I couldn't imagine spending day after day as the only young black kid in a sea of much richer white people. It was hard enough for me to learn how to deal with that in college. What an adolescent had to endure, I can't guess. Because I was the only black man at the school, his mother sought my help. My solution was to suggest that she expose him to successful black families in LA. The boy was obsessed with basketball, so I suggested they hire a young friend of mine, the son of an NBA player, for private lessons. It would give the boy the opportunity to spend time with a prominent, well-respected black family who had plenty of black friends themselves and whose kids had also gone to private school and turned out well. The mother wrote back at length thanking me, but said that they were not like the other families at the school; they weren't rich and couldn't afford the lessons, but that it was valuable for their son to learn that money can't buy the important things in life. Then she added, "Being mixed with rich families is . . . a challenge, but we believe it is also something [he is] learning to deal with."

The uncanny accuracy with which this mother described the anxieties of poorer boys around richer peers was startling. The researchers in both studies I have discussed do not offer much explanation for what they observed. If I were to speculate, I'd say that for adolescent boys social standing means something quite different than it does for girls, and sexuality and dominance play a large part. As the sociologist Eleanor Maccoby has written: "The social structures that emerge in male and female peer groups are different. Male groups tend to be larger and more hierarchical. . . . Boys are more concerned with competition and dominance, with establishing and protecting turf, and with proving toughness, and to these ends they are given to confronting other boys directly, taking risks, issuing or accepting dares, making ego displays, and concealing weakness. Among boys, there is a certain amount of covert sexy (and sexist) talk, as well as the elaboration of homo-phobic themes."[6] In a school with uneven economic stratification—a large number of well-off boys mingling with a smaller number of less-affluent boys—money is a ready sign of dominance. Boys dropped off at school in a BMW and sporting $300 Beats by Dre headphones dominate the smaller number of boys who ride the bus and can afford only a cheap set of earbuds. And in defensive reaction to their feelings of inadequacy, the poorer boys act out, stealing, fighting, "proving toughness . . . making ego displays, and concealing weakness."[7] Despite our thoroughly modern belief in the infinite plasticity of the human mind, aggression and physical strength are a permanent part of the psyche of young boys; when they feel inadequate or insecure or different in some defining way—as poor boys do when they are outnumbered by rich ones—they display that aggression.

I have so far left out any explicit comment on the racial differences of these boys, instead allowing race and financial status to double as easy proxies for one another, as a vast number of black kids in heavily white schools are not as wealthy as their white peers. But my experience in thinly integrated white schools of the type Hannah-Jones described has convinced me that racial differences overlaid on the economic ones add an even more unsettling, and in some ways outright sinister, element to the experience of black boys. And in contemporary times we can trace that element to Mariah Carey and her role in the culture of rap and hip-hop music.

In order to understand that role, a potted history of rap, which is the dominant art form kids are born into today, is first in order here. (Bear with me a little longer. The story of white society's interest in black culture can always be more intricate and perplexing than it may first appear.) Rap was first invented on the streets of New York in the late 1970s. Block parties manned by DJs played popular records on two turntables without a break between songs. Eventually kids without singing talent but who nevertheless wanted to be heard over the records began to chant or vocalize over the beats. In short order the phenomenon of rapping—long, rhyming, mostly playful and boasting chants—was born. People unfamiliar with rap will think that the violence and sexuality and incessant use of the n-word that it is known for today were always a part of the music, but that is untrue. There was always bravado and driving bass beats, but the art form in its first decade would prove nimble and innocent enough to absorb the politically minded (Chuck D and Public Enemy), the prideful and lovelorn (LL Cool J), and those who just wanted to have fun and party (Run DMC). It even expanded, as all lasting art forms must, to include early women rappers (Roxanne Shanté, Queen Latifah). Though the rise of the white artists the Beastie Boys helped give rap some small mainstream appeal, the music was mostly confined to black inner-city radio stations and then slowly moved to black airwaves with wider audiences around the country.

Then the crack epidemic erupted in the late 1980s. And Los Angeles produced its own version of the art form: gangsta rap, full of drugs and gun violence and crude hypersexuality, exploded on the music scene. What had once been a genre that drew the interest of only the black and Latino communities suddenly awakened the appetites of white teen suburbia. As *The New Republic* reported at the time, the advent of SoundScan, a digital tracker that replaced counting album sales by hand, meant that "America awoke on June 22, 1991, to find that its favorite record was not *Out of Time*, by aging college-boy rockers R.E.M., but *Niggaz4Life*, a musical celebration of gang rape and other violence by N.W.A., or Niggaz Wit Attitudes, a rap group from the Los Angeles ghetto of Compton whose records had never before risen above No. 27 on the Billboard charts." The violence and sex of gangsta rap had reached America's white suburban neighborhoods and their prurient interest in the most stereotypical images of black men would prove to be boundless. One adult white writer, commenting on his and his suburban peers' teenage fascination with gangsta rap, wrote that they were mesmerized by what was essentially "ghetto porn," "like something from another planet . . . frightening, confusing and exhilarating."[8] It was "a way," he continued, "of experiencing the thrill of 'otherness'" but in retrospect their obsession with the genre was a "toxic" glorification of violence that harmed the black communities that it erupted from. This toxic interest was just the first destabilizing force injected into black music by whites at the dawn of the twenty-first century. There was more to come.

As gangsta rap grew and the money from the comfortably middle- and upper-middle-class white kids in the suburbs poured into white record companies, many in the black community were naturally alarmed, feeling that a robust and healthy black art form had been hijacked by white kids who were only interested in the most depraved images of black men and women, and the incessant use of the word *nigga* in mainstream culture. But things were about to get worse. One of those suburbanites fascinated with gangsta rap was the pop princess Mariah Carey, born and raised in Suffolk County, New York, in a town that was less than 1 percent black, who was challenging Whitney Houston for the title of top pop diva in the country. After being established as the white counterpoint to Houston during her first album's success, Carey began to speak a bit more openly about her father's mixed heritage and to fortify claims of that ancestry, she began a remarkable transformation. Almost overnight she went from being Mariah Carey, America's reigning white pop princess, to "Mimi," the possibly black-ish, though still white to the naked eye, gangsta rap moll of the late 1990s and early 2000s, appearing in a dozen rap videos, frolicking in skimpy clothing with black rappers, from Ol' Dirty Bastard to Bone Thugz-N-Harmony to Jermaine Dupri. The suggestion of taboo sex between the for-all-intents-and-purposes white Mariah Carey and the "dangerous" black gangsters of rap music meant a stage was being set. A Rubicon was about to be crossed. And yet another toxic destabilization of black culture was underway.

Despite the white-skinned Carey's presence, scantily clad black women (the kind who were black to the naked eye) were still overwhelmingly the main objects of crude objectification in rap, and many leaders in the black community had tired of how wholly black women were being demeaned. Everyone from Al Sharpton to Oprah Winfrey raised urgent concerns about the impact of these images on primarily black kids who were now ingesting them in their living rooms too. The white suburban kids would be fine, the reasoning went. Their two-parent, stable homes in safe neighborhoods, miles away from poor inner-city neighborhoods, would shield them from the negative impact of the images they were consuming; plus, they had famous white people aplenty to model themselves after. But what about the black kids, and black boys especially, who only had famous rappers and athletes to teach them what success looked like?

The fight for greater black female dignity in rap music, in particular, came to a head in 2004 at Spelman College, a historically black women's college. The rapper Nelly had gone there to hold a bone marrow drive for his sister, who was dying of leukemia. But the music video for his sexually explicit song "Tip Drill" could be charitably described as nothing more than soft-core porn. The video had abandoned all pretense of artistry and depicted black women as little more than sexual toys. Upon his arrival on their campus, the women of Spelman erupted.

In the face of the growing national outcry, rappers and record company execs had what some might call an ingenious idea, and Carey's example had cleared the way for it. Rather than reforming the depiction of black women in videos, they simply decided to eliminate black women from their videos altogether and replace them with white women, Latinas, or white-to-the-naked-eye "black" women like Carey. This was the third, destabilizing tremor: the suburban world's excitement around rap kicked into overdrive. White suburban teenagers, who had already been revealed as the primary consumers of gangsta rap and had been treated to Carey coquettishly cavorting with dark-skinned male gangster rappers for several years, glommed onto the wholesale whitening of women in rap. Now this "ghetto porn" that "seemed to be from another planet" that white kids had been so deeply fascinated with seemed to be saying back to them, "We see you too and we are as taken with you as you are with us. We're here to be dangerous thugs solely for your white viewing (and sexual) pleasure." By the early twenty-first century, gangsta rap would become the most popular and far-reaching art form black Americans ever produced and, more, practically no black women would be found in it. (The whitening of women in rap coincided with the gradual disappearance of black female rappers from the genre, who at one point, at the height of the 1990s, dominated the field, with as many as a dozen female artists, from sex kitten Lil' Kim to the politically conscious Lauryn Hill to the tomboy Missy Elliott, turning out hits. Today the biggest female in rap is a white-skinned Latina who only dates black men. Her hit song on the radio right now has her repeating the phrase, "Fuck him and I get some money" over and over. How times have changed.) Carey, by stoking the racist fantasies of white suburban youth, helped Trojan horse the fetish for white women (and white to the naked eye black women) into the very center of black American culture where it had only previously existed on the fringes (where it belongs), and in so doing, drove out black women and their erotic appeal from the previously black art form they helped create and inspire. Rap music would, instead, become almost completely defined by black men pursuing and being pursued by a white-skinned female sexual partner.*

What this transformation meant was that the rappers and record company executives of the new American century, who hold such sway over today's youth culture, devised something that had never before existed in human civilization: an art form in which the male praised and pursued the erotic beauty of a female lover who did not belong to the same tribe or race as the man. In the *Odyssey* the Greek Odysseus longs to return home to his Greek wife. In the *Kama Sutra* the Hindu man pleases his Hindu lover. Navajo men proclaim their love for Navajo women, not Cherokee women. In the love poetry of ancient Egypt, lovers referred to themselves as brother and sister because they were indistinguishable from other members of their tribe. White country music singers (and white pop singers for that matter) proclaim their love for white country lovers, not black or Asian ones. This is not so in rap music.

While this wholesale change is plainly damaging to the self-worth of black girls, what does this tell us about the mind and

---

* I want to be clear that by the word *fetish* I am not referring to whips, chains, and leather, but sexual fixation on a different race's skin color. A white man with "yellow fever" has a racial fetish for Asian women. A white woman who only dates black men has a racial fetish for black men. Unlike whips and chains, race fetish is the opposite of color-blindness and is not only psychologically unhealthy and socially harmful, it is powerfully associated with some of the most vile criminal acts in modern U.S. history. O. J. Simpson and the serial murderer Jeffrey Dahmer both had skin-color fetishes.

behavior of black boys in all-white environments? Well, first, they are following their idols' leads in one obvious way. When I taught at Fairfax High School, a predominantly white school in Hollywood, all the perfectly lovely black girls were without boyfriends (I asked a group of black girls in the class I was teaching), while the black boys paraded proudly through the halls with their white and light-skinned Latina girlfriends. A friend from Ohio was home last year and overheard her niece on the phone wondering about a date to the prom. For several minutes she listened with growing alarm as her daughter and her friends cycled through one black boy after the other, responding with, "No, he only dates white girls. No, he doesn't date black girls. No, he only likes Asians." Another friend in Detroit rejoiced that her daughter was finally graduating and off to Howard University. That year, her daughter and all the other black girls at the high school had no dates to prom. All the white boys took white girls and all the black boys also took white girls. The black girls, who did not want to miss out on a milestone but had no dates, decided to go to the prom as a group.

It is now perfectly commonplace to look at Twitter and see a young black kid openly tweeting his disdain for black girls:

black girls ugly af bruh

I recall seeing an Instagram video some years ago of a dark-skinned black kid, surrounded by all white friends, saying, "This is what I do when a dark-skin black girl passes by." Then a Doberman Pinscher walks down the hall, and the black boy and all his white friends recoil in horror.

But then so what? We're talking about disruptive behavior. Even if black boys leave white schools only being able to see the appeal of white girls and forever disdaining black ones (as too many of them do), does that mean they're misbehaving in white schools too? No, not always, but some are. A black friend who went to a fancy boarding school told me that the few black boys with black girlfriends were looked down on, whereas those who had white girlfriends were not. Another, wiser friend asked whether that was how the white kids felt or how our mutual black friend felt about having a black girlfriend: that it was something to look down on. My point is that the "preference" for white girls is proof of a profound feeling of racial inferiority in black men and boys, and feeling inferior, as the studies and stories I pointed to in the beginning show, is the trigger for bad behavior in boys when they are surrounded by people who are socially "superior" to them in some fundamental way (wealthier, whiter). Some historical proof of this claim can be found once again in the words of Thomas Jefferson.

The late titan of black studies at Duke University, John Hope Franklin, once told me that Jefferson was the Founding Father he liked the least. It was not because Jefferson owned slaves, but because, in addition to being the author of perhaps the greatest document of human freedom ever written, Jefferson, with exquisitely painful irony, also helped to promulgate the ideology that justified enslavement, the ideology of black inferiority. I sought out Jefferson's words on black people. He provided many reasons for his belief in black people's physical, moral, and physiological inferiority to whites, all of which we would find manifestly absurd today, but his most chilling "proof" was devastatingly psychological. He wrote in 1785 in *Notes on the State of Virginia* that it was the black man's "own judgment in favor of [white women], declared by their preference of them [*sic*] . . . [and white women's] superior beauty" that proved black people were inferior to whites. If the black race is truly equal to the white, why do so many black men clearly prefer to sexually combine with white women over the women of their own race? was Jefferson's piercing argument more than two hundred years ago. But Jefferson was wrong, of course, but only by a single word. What that preference, in fact, proves is not that black people are inferior to whites, but that black men with such a preference *believe* black people to be inferior to whites. A prominent black Hollywood actor who grew up in the South once said he was called nigger so much he thought it was his name. Today, he is well known in Hollywood for never dating black women. His children are all half white and he is currently dating a white tabloid celebrity and actress.

And Thomas Jefferson can rejoice in his grave. Because some two hundred years after he wrote those stinging words, black rappers of the twenty-first century, driven by the prurient appetites of white suburban kids, took up his most-shameful mantle, distorting a once-great art form so that it no longer praised the beauty and erotic appeal of the women of their own race—as all art forms have done since the beginning of time—but rather glorified the superior beauty of the white race.

My encounter with how the explosion in the skin-color fetish is tied to errant behavior in black boys was on full and painful display when I worked at Hollywood High School for one day during the first two months of my year of subbing. I was taking the place of a twelfth-grade history teacher. It was the Friday before a three-day weekend, and the teacher had left worksheets for the kids to do. I didn't have to do a second of teaching. Twelfth-graders are usually a dream, no matter what school you're in. If they've made it that far in school, they've pretty much figured things out. They're on their way to adulthood. They want their credits with as little stress as possible and don't have a whole lot of time for nonsense. In other words, it promised to be a perfect day. Most of the seniors, all of whom were white or Asian, were quiet, whether they were doing their work or not. About twenty kids were in the class; the smaller number of girls were clustered on one side of the room, the boys on the other. Mingling with the pack of about eight girls was one white boy in a red baseball cap that he had tipped to the side. About halfway through the class a black student showed up. It was unusual to see black students at this school, which had no black teachers. When we saw each other, it was always a happy surprise even though we were strangers. Black students at white schools love having black teachers. Black teachers at white schools love having black students. But this black kid was a little different; his body language expressed neither surprise nor delight nor much interest in me at all. He was not carrying books or a pass. I had subbed in enough schools to know that being late, with no pass and an unfriendly demeanor, could mean trouble, no matter the student's race or gender. And a tough-looking black kid at an all-white school in an all-white-and-Asian class was a bit new to me this early in my subbing year. In all honesty, I was curious. Even as a successful adult with a Harvard degree, someone who thinks hard about the exigencies of race and has friends of every race across the globe, some of whom number among the most powerful people in the country, I am a bit wary when I enter a room and realize I am the only black person there. How had this seventeen-year-old navigated this setting?

I asked him for his pass. This annoyed him, but he dug in his pocket and fished it out. I asked his name to double-check. I didn't want to single out the only black kid, but if this wasn't his class, it was better to mind the administration's rules. (There are legal liabilities for allowing a student in your classroom who doesn't belong. This was his class; he was just late.) As weird and mystical as this may sound, I was trying to feel my way through what seemed like the press of social forces of which at the time I was not fully aware and did not have within my control. He entered and walked straight past the white and Asian boys, acknowledged none of them, and went immediately to sit with the girls, all of whom were white. The only boy in the girls' group was the white kid dressed like Eminem. Did the black kid not know the boys in the first group? They outnumbered the girls. The handouts were lying on a table at the top of the room, and the directions were written on the board. I decided to bring the work over to him. He paid me only scant attention as I tried to walk him through the work. He nod-ded before I was finished and mumbled, "I got it."

I went back to the teacher's desk. The girls immediately showed their awareness of the student who had just joined them. Some put their work down and started openly chatting with him. Others twirled their hair or tied it in a bun. Flirtatious jokes went back and forth between them. Their corner of the room had gone from quiet to a bit of rowdiness. I didn't single him out, just said, "Hey, guys, keep it down." He and the girls went quiet for a bit.

Eventually the noise level rose again. Nothing ridiculous but it was pointed, almost like a performance, and since some students were busily working, I offered him and his female companions an-other generic "Hey, guys, keep it down. Class will be over soon, but there are people still trying to work." He was the only one who responded, "You doing too fucking much, bruh." I looked at him with a raised eyebrow and said, "What?" In that brief second be-tween my "What?" and what happened next, my mind flashed to something that had happened to me nearly a decade earlier.

I was a guest at a big event thrown by a liberal institution on the East Coast. I was one of only a few black men there, and I do not recall seeing any black women. At one point a black man well-known in the literary world arrived. I recognized him from a pro-file that had appeared in *The New York Times*. I was among the least important of the guests there, and though I was briefly introduced to him, he paid me no attention. At the dinner later that night, as hundreds of well-known people, nearly all of them white, gathered in the dining hall, I went to my table at the back where the other nonfamous invitees were seated. I looked up to see the black guy enter. About ten minutes into the meal, I was chatting with my dinner companions when I felt a hand pat me on the back and heard someone say, "Good to see you, my man." I looked up. It was he. He didn't speak to anyone else at the table. I fumbled out a "Yeah, you too, man" and watched as he moved off, back to his seat clear on the other side of the room. I was confused. What had just happened? Did he realize he had been a little rude to me when we first met and wanted to make up for it by giving me more love as a fellow black man in this room of all white people? Had someone told him I was an aspiring writer and the next literary sensation so he wanted to lay the groundwork for eventually signing me to a million-dollar deal? Or, more likely, had he confused me with someone else? The person to my right asked how I knew him. I was honest and said I didn't really. She then told me she had been sleeping with him for a year. She was white. I remembered the article from *The New York Times* where he was pictured with his wife, who was also white. The woman next to me was not his spouse. Clearly he was challenging me in a contest I didn't know I was in, a casual warning to both me and the woman next to me. She was a white woman bold enough to fuck one married black man with a fetish, and if I had one, what would stop her from trying to fuck me?

And now this young kid, trained by the bipolar white world around him, the giggling white girls, the awestruck, delighted white boys, was doing the same thing. In his youthful mind there was only one version of being a black man, and in that room he was it. And his business that day—to the delight of his audience—was to prove it. To make a long story short, the situation escalated until he said, "Nigga, get the fuck out here." I was still sitting at the desk on the other side of the room when he said it. I asked him, dumbfounded, "What did you just call me?" He responded, "Whatever, dude. I'm black!" I saw red and quietly told him to leave my class.

This would never have been possible prior to the rise of Mariah Carey (and white women) in rap. That a black boy would call a black man well over twice his age a nigga (in anger or in jest) in front of a room full of white people in order to secure the sexual approval of the racist prurient white girls who were watching. As disgusted as I was, it's hard to lay all the blame on him. He was a lone black kid who had found the easiest purchase for a black boy in an all-white environment. The boy gave them their nigger as my brother had done all those years ago without knowing why he had. He wasn't a star athlete (which comes with its own set of valorized racist stereotypes); he wasn't a bona fide nerd, acing every class; he wasn't the class president. He was, I learned from the assistant principal, the son of a single mother who'd transferred him to Hollywood High hoping he'd thrive in a safer, thinly integrated environment. And the role he couldn't help but choose—the black sexually dominant troublemaker whom the white girls wanted to fuck and the white boys were in awe of—was ready-made for him. He gave them their nigger. My presence, which suggested the bankrupt nature of such a role, was something his mind had been trained to reject.

This phenomenon is so sinister because young black boys, in their troubled self-doubt, think they are being flattered by the fetishistic attentions of nonblack women, when they are in fact being demeaned. They feel empowered in so-called integrated environments by the status they believe racialized sexual interest confers on them among other boys and men, both black and white. Kanye West, married to a racial fetishist and quite likely one himself, rapped, "Fuck you and your Hampton house / I'll fuck your Hampton spouse." But it is because *Kanye* believes he is inferior to the white owner of the Hampton house, that *Kanye* is so determined to fuck the "Hampton spouse." But among the talented bad boys of pop culture, who is more lost than Kanye West?

And it will get worse before it gets better. Because the skin-color fetish of the black man as no longer linked erotically with black women but only to white women did not stop with contemporary black music. No. In the past handful of years, the white suburban teens of thirty years ago have become the advertising and record executives of today. And the white, mostly liberal Mad Men of the ad world (only 1 percent of ad executives are black and 70 percent of them vote Democrat), still electrified by the skin-color fetish that started with Mariah Carey, have dragged their fascination with black man–white woman sex into the mainstream of Madison Avenue. In the summer of 2016, MTV premiered a show called *Dating Naked*, which is about exactly what the title says. The billboard advertisement featured a naked, dark-skinned black man on one side and a naked white girl on the other, staring longingly at each other. When *Harper's Bazaar* celebrated its 150th anniversary in 2017, black R&B singer The Weeknd was featured on the cover, flanked on either side by two white women. Inside, he was pictured sitting at a piano with a blonde sitting seductively on top. Another photo shows him surrounded by two white women and a black woman so fair I had to look closely to see that she was black. On Sunset Boulevard near my house, FILA and Urban Outfitters featured a massive ten-foot-tall billboard with a dark-skinned black guy leaning in close to his white blond paramour who was wearing a matching track suit. This was the only interracial couple they featured. During Christmas 2016, MeUndies, the underwear company, depicted a dark-skinned black man wearing only underwear flanked by two white women in bras and panties, tugging at the waistband of his skivvies. MeUndies uses no other type of interracial couples in their ads.

In 2014 Warby Parker, the progressive eyeglass company, released two commercials online. One showed a blond woman in a bikini lounging lazily on a pool float. She drags her finger seductively through the water, calling, "Marco!" to a dark-skinned, bare-chested black lover who yells back, "Polo!" At one point she stretches her arms out in a happy, zombie-like pose as she walks toward him in their flirtatious game of Marco Polo. Another ad showed a black guy named Darius being awakened by a text from someone named Kennedy. As he hunts for his glasses, he stumbles into a room full of white women who sneaked into his house to surprise him on his birthday. *Weird*, I thought. *Black Darius doesn't have any black female friends?** Warby Parker had no other interracial pairings in its advertising that year. At Christmas 2017, Warby Parker sent out a tiny flier with a black man and a white girl wearing matching glasses and leaning in close to each other. It seems the liberals at Warby Parker feast on fetish.

When Louis Vuitton, that most aspirational of brands, cast Jaden Smith, the gender-bending son of Will Smith, as its women's wear model in 2015, *The New York Times* hailed the company's artistic director for his ability to "sense social change and give it form" and to make Vuitton "appear edgy and forward thinking and millennial sensitive."[9] But his ads uniformly featured Jaden Smith with white women. For Madison Avenue, selling high-end luxury means never pairing a black man with a black woman. Gender originality by using Smith, sure, but the same rigid stereotypes for race. (Smith himself, like The Weeknd, has had two girlfriends, both white, one a Kardashian. His most recent girlfriend's previous boyfriend was black, like the Kardashians'. This is not racial originality or color blindness. This is racial fixation, racial fetish.) In the HBO show *Westworld* the black male character was not introduced until the third episode. Several naked white men had appeared but never as full-frontal nudes. As one black Twitter user wrote rather bluntly, "I understand folks are naked all the time on this show, but the minute they introduce the first naked Black man, he's semi-hard and stereotyped. Of course, the narrative surrounding him is how big his dick is, and how his 'assets' will go to waste if he doesn't get placed in the park."[10] As I write this, Ruffles is airing a commercial in which a bumbling

---

* Only when I paused the commercial on YouTube and then made it play slowly did I realize that a few men were standing in the back of the room, but all of them were white, and the video flashes past them so quickly that the eye sees only women.

white guy gets schooled on the basketball court by a black player who, after sinking a basket, points to the sideline, where two white women wave and wink at him.

The fetishistic image of the black male pursuing the white-skinned woman, borrowed from gangsta rap, is now so ubiquitous, so global, that a Chinese laundry company created its own version in the summer of 2016, releasing an ad for detergent in which a ragged, dark-skinned black guy whistles flirtatiously at a Chinese woman. She calls him over suggestively, then pushes him into the washing machine, only to have him reemerge as a "clean" Chinese man. Google can't make it into communist China, but apparently the ironclad rules of color fetishism can. I could easily cite a hundred more of these depictions. The suggestion of fetishistic sex between black men and white women is now used the world over to sell everything from laundry detergent, underwear, eyeglasses, and potato chips to cable television shows and brand-name luggage.

The world that what I think of as "fetish rap"—the black rapper with the inevitably white female paramour—has engendered is so unsettling because while the many private virtues of art cannot be gainsaid, one of the singular public virtues of art is to bind a race of people to themselves. The Homerian Greeks hearing of the Greek Odysseus longing for his home and the bed of his Greek wife gave shape, heft, and pride to Greek identity. This is especially important for oppressed minority cultures who are dominated and outnumbered by more dominant races, as blacks are in the United States. We cherish Walt Whitman for his private exultations ("I celebrate myself"), but as a nation we cherish him for his public ones ("I hear America singing"). Whitman, and artists like him, helped give the Americans of the still young nation a sense of self-worth, praising the unique American "beauty that comes from beautiful blood and beautiful mind." In fact, the entire thematic strain of American art of the eighteenth century through the early twentieth century was to reject the supposedly superior beauty of English art, architecture, topography, and people in favor of the crude, more natural beauty of the American landscape, to bind (admittedly, white) American citizens to themselves against the tyranny of their British colonizers. And that is as it should have been. Imagine, then, if the Yoruba, alone in the history of the world, had manufactured an art form in which Yoruba men turned away from the beauty of Yoruba women, the women of their own tribe, in order to glorify exclusively the beauty of Igbo women (while Igbo men continued to celebrate Igbo women, their own women, too), and it became the most lasting art form the Yoruba tribe ever created. What would become of Yoruba women? What would become of Yoruba people? What would it tell us about how Yoruba men and boys felt about being Yoruba?

Or, better yet, imagine if the tiny population of Sephardic Jews in seventeenth-century Spain, after centuries of pressure to spurn Judaism, after centuries of Christian dogma that claimed Jews had hook noses and devil horns, had begun to dedicate Jewish love poems to Christian women? And as those poems reached Christian ears, they were taken up with delight and spread by Christian powers to every corner of Europe? And the Jewish poets who gloried in the superior beauty of Christian women were rewarded with fame and glamour and a hearty welcome in the halls of power and prestige? And for decades young Jewish boys, like all boys, followed the habits of the successful and powerful men of their tribe in seeking status and wealth and glory in a world that typically despised their people and turned away from Jewish women for the erotic affections of Christian ones? And those poems also became the most popular, the most globally dominant and influential art form the Jews ever invented? What would have become of Jews?

This is not an idle analogy. This is the world black youth are being raised in. For roughly ten years now white consumers (and willing black producers), electrified by a skin-color fetish, have doubled down on this rigid sexual typing—providing a broader welcome to the perversions of the racialized mind than at any time since the antebellum period while pretending that what we are witnessing is only color-blind diversity in action. Some may tell you that promoting black men and white women together in casually sexual ways is an anodyne or even salutary turn in American life. I think it is as corrupt and racist a turn as we have ever seen. And it will get worse before it gets better. And this is surely what alarmed Beyoncé Knowles when, describing the thinking behind her acclaimed album *Lemonade*, she remarked that it seemed as if black men and women today are being socialized to *not* be together. Or when the rapper Nicki Minaj said more bluntly, "All the rappers are dating blondes. Who is gonna tell black girls they're pretty?" The growth of fetish rap has rendered black women increasingly sexually lifeless, sexually inert, in the eyes of black boys and men.

Even as an all-white, mostly liberal Madison Avenue (inspired, to be sure, by black racial fetish rappers like Kanye West, Big Sean, and any number of southern rappers) was sexually stereotyping black men, the United States was witnessing an outbreak of racist violence against black men by white cops. In the white American mind the hypersexualized black man has always been the ugly twin of the hyperviolent black man. That these things erupted together—the killings of Trayvon Martin, Philando Castile, Eric Garner, and an ever-increasing number of unarmed black men by overtly racist (no doubt politically conservative) cops and the overt sexualization of black men linked to white-skinned women by covertly racist (liberal) image makers should come as no surprise. In his National Book Award–winning study, *Stamped from the Beginning*, the scholar Ibram Kendi shows how, from the earliest days of the European colonies, racist ideas around sex, intelligence, and aggression have been a part of how whites have viewed (and hunted) the black male body. In 1526 an Italian writer published an account of the African continent, writing, "[There] is no nation under Heaven more prone to Venery [sexual indulgence]. . . . [They] leade a beastly kind of life, being utterly destitute of the use of reason." Shakespeare's first black character, Aaron, as Kendi points out, is "evil and oversexed."[11]

Young black boys now grow up in a society in which they see two dominant images of themselves: one in which one type of white person (the Kardashian clan) apparently targets their skin color for sexual purposes, and one in which another type of white person (George Zimmerman) apparently targets their skin color for violent purposes. Their own untutored instincts and low self-image (and the explosion of fetish rap) encourage them to embrace the first while denouncing the second. Many have no fathers in their lives to tell them that the sexual interests of Kim Kardashian and the violent interests of George Zimmerman are one and the same, the terrible fruit of a single poisoned tree.

Perhaps you doubt how viciously locked together (and ubiquitous) this grotesque cycle of skin-color fetish and violence toward black men is, or perhaps you will even say that the seemingly growing number of white women like Kim Kardashian who openly fetishize black men, in some strange way, evens things out? Surely they do it because they worship and feel inferior to the black race? Not even close. White women fetishize black skin knowing full well the "superior" standing the racist world accords them and the potential danger it foments against black men. And they delight in it. I'll end with this message I saw on Twitter last year. A black kid, in London no less, tweeted out a message his friend had received from a white girl who wanted to sleep with him. She was drunk and the friend was uninterested. She became increasingly agitated as he ignored her demands for sex, ultimately kicking her out without giving her what she wanted. Her texts turned hostile at some point, insisting that if he did not comply she would accuse him of rape.

STAMPED FROM THE BEGINNING   105

Girl: they will believe me, you're black, it's in your nature to

Girl: gorilla boy

Girl: wog boy, let me be your wog socket

Girl: I'm white, the police will believe me

Girl: even if you screenshot this convo, they won't care, they want you blackies to rot in prison

Wog is London slang for *nigger,* of course. Everything in American life (and beyond) is conspiring to tell black boys that they are by their nature different, and less than, even if the surge of sexual fascination with them seems to them like power and glamour. In American society the only route to freedom for black boys who are struggling toward manhood is and always will be to reject those who both fetishize and demonize them, to confer a plague on both their houses. Fortifying the struggling schools in black neighborhoods to speed black boys on their way is more important than ever. Sending them to thinly integrated white schools, where they must contend with the perceptions of both conservative and liberal whites who refuse to cure their own minds of racial hate and racial fantasies, which are, of course, one and the same, is to doom these boys to a forest of poison-tipped thorns they can barely survive. When they are lucky, black girls have a delicate sorcery that can help them emerge from these schools intact. But girls cannot easily transfer this gift to their brethren. Boys are left to run this gauntlet alone. Growing into a healthy-minded black man today is, for black boys, an exact and punishing science, and all too many people in the world around them are setting them up to fail.

6

The Child Is Father to the Man

You can learn a lot in middle school. One day in early November I was at a middle school that feeds into Cullen. I'd been subbing over two months and in some ways I felt like a pro; in other ways I was as lost as ever. My brain is such that I'd long since realized that when it comes to race there are often two dramas playing out in front of me, the one you see and the one you don't see. But then maybe it's not just about race. Maybe it's just basic human psychology: The man greeting his wife at the airport with a bouquet of roses seems happy to see her, but the truth is she hates roses and he knows it. He's been cheating on her with a mistress who loves roses. Maybe the wife cheated first, and he's found the right way to turn the knife as he greets her in the most passive-aggressive way possible. I'm a preacher's son, and in the book of Ephesians, Paul says to his followers, "For we wrestle not against flesh and blood but against principalities. Against powers. Against the rulers of the darkness of this world."[1] Growing up and hearing that more than a few times, I think, trained my mind to wonder: What's really going on here? I'd have made a good shrink. But instead it's made me a decent substitute teacher. And a curious one.

Daylight saving time had just came a few days before, as I woke in the cold dark of my apartment on this particular November morning. The extra hour of sleep felt sweeter than it had ever felt. I'd gotten at least a few days' work booked in advance each week, once my reputation for being tough and getting the work completed started to spread. This meant that the phone didn't ring as much in the morning, but the house was colder and darker when it did. The ride from Hollywood into South LA is harder in November. I was part of the zombie class of workers up before the sun. I'd gotten pretty comfortable standing in front of a group of strangers, although the sense of vertigo derived from the fact that my day-to-day life could look so different from one morning to the next—one day an Orthodox Jewish academy in West LA, the next morning a working-class Christian charter in East LA—never fully went away.

I'd also become more at ease with my role as a hard-ass. I liked it, in fact. "We need more mean teachers," Mr. Yancy, the art teacher at Cullen, told me one day, and I heartily agreed. Students continued to try me, and I could still get thrown for a loop by some kid who suddenly exploded in the middle of class (like the kid at Hollywood High), but by then I was giving as good as I got and I won most skirmishes. I also was smarter about which kids to challenge and which ones to leave alone.

Nothing had rattled me quite like the kid at Hollywood High. *Angered* is probably more accurate. I wanted to bash his face in. When I spoke with the assistant principal (a black male, as it turned out), the kid ticked all the boxes on the usual, distressing demographic checklist: single mom, no dad in the picture. It got me to thinking about, among other things, how fatherlessness has helped prime the earth for the widespread growth of skin-color fetish in rap because black boys grow up without seeing dads showing respectful, erotic affection to black women, so they take cues from the next best thing: famous rappers and athletes. "You must be a man yourself before you try to train a man; you . . . must set the pattern he must copy," Rousseau says of fathers in *Emile*.[2] Role modeling matters.

But it's not all that matters, and it may not even be the most important thing when it comes to what I came to see as the very unusual purpose a father serves for his son. I was thinking about that dynamic, as old as Creon, king of Thebes, as I headed to the middle school in South LA. During my first period, I was listening to a few seventh-grade boys talk. The biggest kid was Kevin. He wasn't talking loudly, but I could hear him pretty clearly. He was nervous, he said, about going to see his dad on the weekend because when his dad got upset with him he'd punch Kevin in the chest. Hard. His father once punched him so hard it knocked the wind out of him. "I couldn't catch my breath for, like, a hour. I thought I was gonna die for real." One of his friends, Deontae, nodded solemnly. His dad had done the same to him. Substitutes, as I understand it, are not mandatory reporters of child abuse, but it didn't matter. Even if we were, I wouldn't have called the authorities. Despite the fearful talk, I was actually charmed. I happened to know that Kevin and Deontae weren't really upset; they were actually proud. The two of them were humble-bragging about how strong their fathers are. "Man, my dad let me punch him in the chest once," Deontae said. "I tried to run and punch him. But he didn't even move. He just stood there. When he punched me though, man, it hurt." I know this game. I played it as a kid and I know plenty of other boys who did, too. For some reason getting punched in the chest by your dad until you lose your breath is a magical experience for prepubescent boys. For them, how strong their fathers are matters a lot, to their sense of masculinity, dominance, even their sense of safety.

Adult black men conducted a similar conversation on Twitter with the same sense of amused pride. But it was qualitatively different too. A Twitter user asked his followers, "Fellas, what age were you when you bucked up against the male authority figure in your life?" The responses, all from black men, were uniformly hilarious, though some were hairier than others. One tweeter replied:

> My step pop was a 4th degree black belt and always told us "you don't like something we can go outside" I never tried him. Lol

A second said:

> Pops was mad the crew & I were being loud while playing Mortal Kombat. I disagreed. Got choked off my feet in front of the whole crew.

Yet another wrote:

> Bruh my dad had a major stroke last year and right side was paralyzed. His left side still strong as FUCK. Im good.[3]

But the best response came from a tweeter who had, as his avatar, a picture of him holding the hand of his tiny, barely standing son, who was dressed like Paddington Bear. A picture in the background was of the tweeter as a boy sitting on his father's lap.

> bucked at dad, got punched in my chest so hard it knocked the wind out of me, thought I was dying. Still believe he's the best dad ever.[4]

A final respondent brought the point home:

> feeling myself bc I was taller than dad @ 13, caved my chest in came to my senses on the kitchen floor w/boot on chest, still my best friend.[5]

As I thought about the connection between the young boys and the adults, all of whom were recounting the same type of admiring affection they had for physically strong father figures, I had what can only be described as an epiphany. Role modeling may be important, but there is a far more important and elemental part adult men play in a young boy's development. All kids (boys and girls) eventually test the adults in their lives, but I now believe the outcome of that test, for boys especially, goes to the heart of the real dangers of fatherlessness. I recalled hearing a similar story from a black sports reporter on the radio. He was young. His parents had divorced and his mother hadn't yet remarried. One day he was "feeling himself" and said something cheeky to her. She was much smaller than he was, but she still went after him. That was the last time he tested her. But it seemed to me that something was different about the black reporter's story. As I thought about all those stories, I began to understand why the great numbers of black men absent from the lives of their sons lead to such chaotic behavior in boys.

Although the reporter's mother got him back in line, he was by then taller and stronger than she was and wasn't in any physical danger. But he was big enough to hurt her. The reporter's yielding to his mother's authority in that moment was loving and respectful but also, in some way, purely voluntary. But speak reckless to your father at thirteen and you might get choked off your feet right in front of your friends. And that, I believe, matters in the mind of an adolescent boy and makes a massive, life-changing difference.

A crucial, if unconscious, change occurs in the mind of a fatherless son, especially in a community of fatherless sons, when he realizes he can physically topple his authority figure, that is, his female parent. When he hits puberty and he is suddenly his mother's size, more agile than she, with more muscle mass, and growing bigger and taller than she with each passing day, he begins to no longer fear her physical dominance; when he sees that he can hurt her (and she sees it too), that he can subdue, or in the most primal sense, kill her, a boy suddenly thinks of himself differently than he did before. He thinks of himself, even if unconsciously, as a man. The only authority figure above him can no longer hurt him.

Let me provide more examples. The sixteen-year-old student I mentioned in chapter 2, who threatened me after I asked about his homework, pounding his fist into his hand and saying, "What you gon do? What you gon do? We both grown men. We both grown men," is one. I believe he was testing his manhood, in front of his peers, against me. The principal (who'd come to respect me and saw how upset I was by the incident) sent him home for a day and a half and he was only able to return with his parent—his mother. There was no father or uncle in the picture. As we sat in the office with his mother and the assistant principal trying to get the student to apologize to me and acknowledge that what he'd done was out of line, his mother tried everything she could to cajole him— smiling at him, complimenting him, lightly chastising him, trying to make him laugh—to say he was sorry, but he sat there angry and unmoved. Only after being told that he wouldn't be re-admitted to school did he offer a half-hearted apology. His mother was half his height and body weight, and he could've crushed her with a single blow. This sixteen-year-old had clearly wrenched away the physical monopoly of power from his mother, and now she was left in the role of trying to charm and gently persuade her son to do what she wanted him to do. After his mother left, I saw him in the hall, and, in an attempt to bury the hatchet (despite not knowing why there was even a hatchet in the first place), I tried to shake his hand, but he waved my hand away and scowled like he was dismissing his servant.

If he had a father he knew living at home, his adolescent brain would have at some point driven him to test his father's physical strength, maybe even at an earlier age. And more likely than not he would've lost that test, and like the Twitter users, realized, as he rolled on the ground with the wind knocked out of him, that he was not yet a man. Imagine, if you're black or come from a working-class background, and you knew what would happen if you aggressively approached your dad or any grown man at fifteen, pounding your fist in anger and saying, "We both grown men. We both grown men. What you gon do? What you gon do?" But now that this kid was plainly stronger and more physically dominant than the head of his household, his mother, his brain told him he was a "grown man" and ready to challenge the other men around him.

My brother tells a story of a kid who entered his tattoo shop with his mother. The mother spoke first, asking how old one had to be to get a tattoo. My brother said eighteen. She asked a few more questions and then turned to her son and said, "It's your tattoo, do you want to talk?" The boy responded, "Yeah, cuz you asking all these dumb questions." My brother blanched and said, "It's not a dumb question." The boy responded, "If I say she asking a dumb question, she asking a dumb question." My brother ignored it. The kid said he wanted a tattoo of his name. My brother counseled against it, saying it was a kinda corny tattoo to get. The boy made some smart remark to my brother, who, fed up at that point, kicked the boy out of his shop. (He still gets angry when I remind him of this story.) As the boy left with his mother, he proceeded to berate her. I asked my brother how big the boy was in comparison to his mother; he was several inches taller. Though I've never met this kid, I feel certain of one thing: there was one fear this kid did *not* have—the fear that when he got home he would be greeted at the door with the angry, coiled fist of a man, his father, in a rage over how his wife had been disrespected in public by their eighteen-year-old son.

When I told a friend this story, a lightbulb went off for her. She instantly recalled an experience, years ago in college, when a male friend told her a story about how he had been talking slick to his mother as a teenager. After crossing one line too many, his father, who had been quietly reading the newspaper, flicked the edge of the paper down and eyed his son. Within a matter of seconds, his father reached into his pocket and hurled a knife through the air, right past the boy's ear, to land in the wall behind him. A clear, very old-fashioned southern warning that there was one king in this man's castle, that his wife was to be respected, and that the child came for either crown at his peril. What amazed my friend at the time was the pride with which her college friend recounted the memory. Like the pride of the seventh-graders I had taught, admiring their fathers who had knocked the wind out of them, and the pride of the grown black men on Twitter who, after describing how their father choked them off their feet for "bucking" against them and talking reckless in front of their friends, pronounced their dads to be their best friends.

I imagine that intellectuals for whom strength, gender, and dominance are all antiquated social constructs without any inherent meaning might blanch at this. I am hardly advocating for knife play, but the physical dominance of an adult male, especially in working-class and poor communities where men in the parenting role are scarce, is crucial to the healthy development of boys as they enter puberty and come to realize (if just subconsciously) that they can physically topple the women above them.

This tremulous mother-son dynamic (an opposite one, in some way, to Freud's Oedipal complex) doesn't just operate in the mind of the child. The mother, I believe, deeply senses it too. The female gangsta rapper Remy Ma tells a hilarious story that points at this. After she had served seven years in prison for shooting a woman she thought had stolen from her, she was released. A radio interviewer asked whether, now that she was out of prison, she had to check her son, as if to say to him, "Like, yo, I'm mommy." She replied:

Naw, he's not like that. He's not disrespectful. But the first time he came to see me [in prison] and . . . I hadn't seen him in two to

three months . . . and he was bigger. I was like [simulating pointing her finger in his face] "Yo! I will wash you!" He was like, "But
I didn't even do anything." [She told him:] "You got bigger than
me! Don't get crazy! You do anything crazy, I got two brothers. I
know they your uncles, but they ride with me first. I will call
them. I will have you washed."[6]

Witness the cause for her surge of anxiety: her adolescent son had
gotten bigger than she was. And where once she could have easily
"washed" him herself, she now needed her brothers in case he got it
in his mind to do anything "crazy." Even a female gangsta rapper
with a fearsome reputation felt a swell of existential panic when her
fourteen-year-old son was too big for her to physically dominate.

But this doesn't happen with boys who are raised with their
fathers in the home. It takes a long time for a boy to be able to challenge his father or father figure and stand any chance of winning.
Note the trigger in the last tweet: "Feeling myself bc *I was taller
than dad @ 13*." This is as primal a challenge as the human animal
is capable of—testing the head of the clan because your size con-
vinces you that you are ready to do so. But by and large in a healthy
home it happens only once (as the tweeters pointed out). Talk too
recklessly to your dad in certain households, and you will awaken
from a brief loss of consciousness gasping for air and with a boot
on your chest. The combination of financial dependence and relative physical weakness means a (healthy) boy bucks his dad once
and only once. And the experience tells his unformed subconscious
mind that he is not yet a man, prolonging his maturation, subduing his aggression, deflating his self-regard. When we add to the
experience of fatherlessness the slightly Freudian element of
husbandless black mothers who "love their sons but raise their
daughters," a common saying in the African American community,
we understand how boys can begin to believe themselves to be
adults before they are ready.

I want to provide an additional anecdote in this regard that powerfully and—I think—beautifully sums up the point I have been making about the primal role men play in dominating and reining in a boy's expanding egoed self. It's from a book called *Are Black Men Doomed?* The sociologist Alfred Young had interviewed men in inner-city Chicago to detail the struggles of poor and working-class black men. One in particular, named Smittie, worked a low-paying job and had taken on the role of father figure for his sister's four sons—the only adult male relative in the boys' lives. One day one of his nephews was in a rage over a kid who'd stolen ten dollars from him. The nephew had gotten his hand on a gun and was determined to kill the boy who'd robbed him. Smittie tried to intervene, to stop his nephew from making an irrevocable mistake:

> I had to actually drive him down on the ground physically. He had a gun. He was gonna shoot somebody over ten dollars. This was Sunday yesterday. And I'm trying to tell him, you know you're reacting, you're not thinking. You know, and I took the gun, you know. He actually bucked [that word again!] up at me. He wanted to fight, and I'm looking at him and I'm saying I see myself in him. . . . Over ten dollars. So what did I do? I took the gun from him. Gave him ten dollars and kicked him out. Told him I don't want to talk to him anymore.[7]

This brief account touches on everything I have been describing in this book. It contains the perfect mixture of stringency and love: driving the boy to the ground, wresting the gun from him, freely giving him (a hard-earned) ten dollars. But also the smart outcasting of the boy and telling him he didn't want to talk to him ever again. Mothers, by and large, cannot wrest a gun from an angry and determined teenage boy's hand. Mothers cannot drive an angry and determined teenager to the ground when he bucks up at her. Smittie's physical strength was an absolutely necessary component (along with the economic means to spare ten dollars) to saving his nephew's life, to subduing his adolescent ego and rage.

So how did this story end? What became of the nephew and the kid who robbed him? Smittie continues,

> And then [my nephew] came back, later on about nine or ten o'clock, "I'm sorry. I won't do that no more." I told him "You know, you don't react. You think first. There's a lot of goddamn hump in the ground out there in [the] cemetery from people reacting and not thinking."

This practically moved me to tears because of how desperately it pointed to the need for fathers and how painfully absent they have been for so long. Boys come to love the men who lovingly subdue them and they eventually grow into men who properly and lovingly subdue their sons.

As a side note, I think it is no coincidence that so few of the most graphic and explicit gangsta rappers had close relationships with their fathers. In their minds they became men the moment they realized they were physically stronger than their mothers. And the things that adolescents crave—sex, money, violent physical dominance over other men—are the things they crave when they actually become adults. It is also no coincidence that the most successful black rappers in the United States right now are Kendrick Lamar and Chance the Rapper, both politically conscious, psychologically complex men from entirely different socioeconomic backgrounds who grew up with their dads in their lives. A responsible (and physically stronger) father delays a boy's unconscious belief that he is an adult (just as the father's presence delays his daughter's acceleration into menarche), because the young male can't yet physically topple the adult above him. And with any luck, by the time the boy can, his mind is preparing him to dominate his own children in lovingly healthy ways.

A final anecdote: the story of a great artist and a friend provides a valuable answer. Let's call him Satchel. As a child, living in New Jersey, he received a bike for his ninth birthday. He was over the moon. With the forgetful excitement of any kid who has gotten his first bike, he rode and rode until, quite innocently, he had crossed into a tougher part of town. He stopped at a light and was preparing to turn toward home when he was approached by two boys a bit older than he. One of them said, "What you doing with my boy's bike?" Satchel was perplexed.

"It's my bike," he responded.

"Naw," one of the boys insisted. "You got my man's bike." In the innocent confusion of a kid who didn't realize he was being shaken down, Satchel tried to explain to them that he had gotten it for his birthday. They weren't interested in his explanation, of course, and the two of them were capable of taking it away from him, and they had every intention of doing so. Satchel, uncertain how to proceed and beginning to panic about how to make them understand that the bike really belonged to him, realized his father probably hadn't yet left for work. So with the perfect earnestness of a nine-year-old, he said, "My dad bought it for me. He's home now. We can go ask him if you want." Satchel told me something remarkable happened: the boys went quiet and took their hands off his bike. "And they let me go." The mere invocation of a male authority seemed to quiet these adolescents bent on relieving Satchel of his bike. He had a fancy new bike, so they of course assumed an adult had purchased it for him, but they hadn't reckoned that the buyer was a man, a father. Men don't just dominate their own sons in healthy ways—they dominate other people's sons in healthy ways too. *Uncle Tyrone might not've been your uncle, but he was the uncle for the neighborhood,* Jay-Z said. When men have been absent from a community for too long, a community of boys believe they are men before their time.

Their story illustrates an important fact: despite the dire statistics about absent fathers, male surrogates can play the same salutary role. In Danielle Allen's *Cuz*, her fifteen-year-old cousin Michael has been sent to an adult prison so far away from his mother, Karen, that she could not visit. With some effort the author is able to get Michael transferred to a prison closer to home.

> Karen could see Michael starting to change in Centinela, not in physical appearance but in his demeanor. He was gaining in confidence and settling down. He . . . overcame his stammer. He converted to Islam. . . . He would tell [his mom] that he was hanging out with the older men who were lifers and that they were taking care of him. She met one of those men once, during a visiting day, and then happened to bump into him years later on the outside. He told her then, "Your son is a good son, he just got caught up." These older black inmates kept Michael focused. He did a lot of reading with them and spent time in the library.[8]

Elephant societies, remarkably similar to human societies, rely on adult males in similar ways:

> As a result of . . . social upheaval, [elephant] calves are now being born to and raised by ever younger and inexperienced mothers. Young orphaned elephants, meanwhile, that have witnessed the death of a parent at the hands of poachers are coming of age in the absence of the support system that defines traditional elephant life. "The loss of elephant elders," Bradshaw told me, "and the traumatic experience of witnessing the massacres of their family, impairs normal brain and behavior development in young elephants." . . . When South African park rangers recently introduced a number of older bull elephants into several desta-

bilized elephant herds in Pilanesberg and Addo, the wayward behavior—including unusually premature hormonal changes among the adolescent elephants—abated.[9]

Sending in bull elephants to calm the swollen herds of younger male elephants was a brilliant fix and, likewise, one solution to the problem of absentee fathers in the black community is more black men teaching in public schools, especially in middle schools. During his presidency Barack Obama inaugurated an effort to recruit more black male teachers but it produced few dividends. I considered this such a serious matter that, in mid-2016, I suggested in an article for *The New Yorker*'s website that Barack Obama should himself consider becoming a part-time public school teacher in his post-presidency:

> In 2013, less than two percent of public-school teachers were black men, which tells us that the overwhelming majority of kids, both black and white, have little direct exposure to professional black men in their daily lives. This has had a disastrous effect on the development of black students, and especially black boys, contributing to their staggering levels of behavioral issues, suspensions, and, ultimately, dropouts. . . . I think Obama should teach, for one year, for even just part of the time, in an inner-city K–12 public school. . . . [The] problems are not straightforward—neither poverty nor racism nor the depredations of popular culture represent a single answer—but Obama, as a high-school teacher, could reinvigorate efforts to solve them.[10]

I stand by that suggestion today.

The role of fathers in boys' lives—and parents in kids' lives—is, of course, a complex one and not always easily understood. And even when a father is present, he does not healthily dominate his child. The book *Nurture Assumption* argues forcefully that peers play a larger role in how a child develops than perhaps even parents do. Whatever the chain of influence, however, most of us can agree that in schools today, whether rich or poor, too many parents have helped to undermine the authority of teachers, enabling children's growing lack of respect for teachers. The child's rights movement, combined with the increasing wealth of Western nations, means that many children have become living luxury items, as coddled and cared for as miniature poodles. A popular cartoon I've seen in many teachers' lounges has one panel, dated 1960, in which parents are yelling at their terrified son for failing a test. In the second panel, a set of more modernly dressed parents are also angry over the failed test, but this time they're yelling at a terrified teacher. This may seem silly, obvious, and mundane, but the question of uncooperative parents goes to the heart of the relationship between a democratic citizen and the state and requires all of our attention.

In his book *The Rule of Nobody* Phillip Howard tells the story of a suburban science teacher living and working in Colorado who had assigned her classes to write an essay. One student turned in the assignment late, and in accordance with her long-standing rule, she took 10 percent off the tardy student's grade. The student's father, a lawyer, was not pleased and when the teacher refused to raise the grade, the father threatened a lawsuit. He dragged the teacher to meeting after meeting. The principal, who did not want to agitate the father, refused to intervene on the teacher's behalf. Howard writes, "After 30 days of sleepless nights, left unsupported by administration, [the teacher] finally capitulated and raised the grade. 'Life's too short,' she said. 'I just can't keep going with this.'"

My own encounter with an uncooperative father came in late November at Cullen. I hadn't subbed there in a few weeks. As I entered the building, I waved hello to Mr. Titus, the assistant principal, whom I'd come to respect. He always supported my efforts to work with tough students, and he was one of the few black male administrators I had seen in charter schools. My fifth period was a free period, which is planning time for teachers. Free periods are a tiny miracle in a substitute's day, an oasis in the blistering desert, unless the administration asks you to cover another teacher's class, which usually feels like a stab in the gut. The bell for fifth period had rung when I heard a knock at the door. I assumed I was going to be sent to a class that was missing a teacher. But the campus aide told me the assistant principal wanted to see me. A sub being summoned to the principal's office is almost never a good thing.

When I arrived, Mr. Titus waved me into his office, where a man, about forty years old, was sitting. Sitting next to him was his stepson, Rodiney. Knucklehead Rodiney. Apparently, he had been acting up in a few classes, but the teachers who had complained about his behavior were busy teaching, so Titus asked me to speak with Rodiney's father. Rodiney and I had reached a thaw in our icy relationship, but Titus wanted the perspective of another adult who had interacted with Rodiney. I was ready to exonerate him for any misbehavior in my class, but the stepfather spoke up before I could say anything. "I don't know this man," he said. "How do I know if he's gonna lie or not?" Titus tried to defend me, saying, "This man is a professional."

"It's teachers who lie. I went to school here. Teachers lie on kids all the time," the man said flatly. Rodiney shifted uncomfortably and stared at the wall.

As a friend of mine who has worked in education for a long time told me, rebuking teachers is a form of empowerment for parents. Unlike members of law enforcement or people in other positions of power, teachers and school administrators are the only authorities with whom parents can come into contact on a regular basis and defy or chastise without suffering consequences. If they've been denied a driver's license or had their car ticketed, there's not much yelling can do for them. But threatening a principal with a lawsuit or calling a teacher a liar can get things done. Parents not only get the satisfaction of beating "The Man" but concrete results such as raised grades and canceled detentions. Schools, principals, and teachers need cooperation with parents, not conflict. And recreating a culture in which teachers are seen as allies rather than as adversaries will take effort. How we go about securing that relationship goes to the heart of what it means to be a citizen of a modern nation.

The three most controversial pieces of legislation from the last thirty years have been the recent tax reform bill, the 2012 healthcare reform, and Bill Clinton's welfare reform. The last two asked an important civic question as each tried to balance what the state can ask of citizens in return for receiving a benefaction from the government. This question—essentially the social contract—has animated every Enlightenment thinker from John Locke to Thomas Hobbes. Healthcare reform, after much debate over such issues as whether obese people should have to pay a higher premium than those who eat healthy and exercise, settled on allowing insurance companies to charge higher premiums for smokers, while also encouraging incentives for exercising. Welfare reform, dubbed workfare, argued that the poor should have to work to receive benefits from the government. (I concede there are controversies surrounding both provisions.) Charter districts, citing the importance of parental engagement for a child's success, began their entry into the public sphere by requiring that parents volunteer in schools a few hours each semester. The American Civil Liberties Union (ACLU) has challenged those requirements, stating that they create a burden on the poor, and has been mostly successful in dismantling them. I happen to think all schools should be able to make some basic request of parents, rich and poor, in exchange for such heavily subsidized education from the state. But that's my take on things, based on my knowledge of the impact of parents, and neither I nor the ACLU should be dictating education policy alone any more than the National Rifle Association alone should be dictating the scope of the Second Amendment. These debates are too central and too important to the nature of our democracy to leave them to one powerful faction or another. A muscular debate is long overdue about the basic level of obligation parents owe the state, if any, for providing their child an education. And, of course, one about the quality of the education the children should be getting in exchange for that obligation. This is what citizenship means.

As I left Rodiney with his dad and Mr. Titus, I headed out of the office to get a quick bite before lunch. But as I was leaving the building, Mr. Titus caught up with me. "Sorry about all that back there. Not all of the parents are that tough to deal with." I told him I was glad to hear it and that Rodiney and I had been getting along lately. He then asked me if I was interested in a long-term assignment at the school. I wasn't. I hemmed and hawed, trying to find the best way to say no. He told me that he'd like the students to see more African American men around campus. He knew right where to stick the knife; I'd been thinking about that same thing, of course. I just didn't mean seeing more of *me* around campus. The assignment, Mr. Titus told me, would be for Ms. Hand's tenth-grade World History class; she was going on sick leave. I didn't ask why but wondered if it was for exhaustion (that was the eventual rumored cause for her absence). She was a first-year teacher, and I had subbed enough at Cullen by then to know that she was having a tough time. The assignment, Titus said, would start right after Christmas and last for at least three months, until the week before spring break, when the tenth-graders had to take the California High School Exit Examination (CAHSEE), the basic skills test required for graduation. He said they were hoping to hire a permanent teacher by spring break, but if they didn't, the assignment would last through the end of the school year. It sounded even less appealing after he told me that. He went on to say that he'd also want me to help some of the seniors who hadn't passed the CAHSEE improve their study skills. There'd be lesson plans for me to start with, but eventually I'd have to come up with more of my own.

All of this pointed to a chorus of "nos" resounding in my head, but I didn't let on right away. Titus offered to pay me more money. I told him that I didn't really care about that. I just didn't know if I was up for being a full-time teacher. I didn't tell him, but I liked the freedom of coming and going as I pleased. He then said, "Some of the kids asked for you." That surprised me. My face must've shown it because he said, with a chuckle, "You're definitely our most popular sub." I smiled too. There's something funny about being a popular sub. He insisted that he didn't want to put someone brand new in the class who couldn't relate to the kids. "Or who's scared of them," he said. "And I know how much they respect you." He knew which buttons to push, and he was pressing them hard.

Perhaps he was pulling my leg about students asking for me; but then again, it's surprising how quickly you can bond with students. I told Titus I'd have to get back to him. He gave me his card and told me to call as soon as I knew something. I already knew I was going to say no; I just wanted to be polite and let him down easy. Over the next few days, the idea of taking on the class didn't enter my mind.

Maybe it was Dayshawn and Greg, and a few other kids, like Clarice, asking me directly, the next time I was booked at Cullen, if I was going to be their teacher next semester. Maybe it was because I worried about what it would mean for the gems and knuckleheads if someone brand new, someone scared of the kids and not a hard-ass, took over the class. Maybe it was because I started to feel an inkling of what people referred to as a "calling" to teach. Whatever it was, by the time I picked up the phone at the end of the week and called Mr. Titus to tell him I couldn't accept the assignment, I ended up leaving a voicemail telling him that as long as he made a strong effort to find someone permanent for the last half of the school year, I'd be willing to take on the job full time.

And with that, the die was cast.

CROSSING THE RUBICON

I went home to my mother's house for Christmas. I was starting to feel that I'd made a terrible mistake—that in just a few weeks I'd be a full-time teacher, completely responsible for a classroom of tenth-graders at Countee Cullen, and I simply wasn't prepared. I'd never thought of teaching full time when I first started subbing: rather, my intent was rising early a few days a week as a way to force me to better organize my life. But something had happened in the process. The strange combination of civic duty my parents instilled in me, my natural curiosity and concern for the world I was being increasingly drawn into, and, frankly, the fact that I enjoyed teaching (even on days I was royally cursed out, provided those days were few and far between) had brought me to the point where I'd be the sole person in charge of guiding a roomful of gems, knuckleheads, and assholes in a tenth-grade World History class for at least three months. All I wanted to do was back out, but it was too late.

At home, eating my mother's food and sleeping on my mother's couch, I asked her advice from a lifetime of teaching. She was happy to know I too was teaching now, even though I had kept from her the worst of what I'd experienced. I didn't want to worry her too much. She had always encouraged me to be a teacher, but I was not nearly as excited about it as she. Schools had changed since she had worked full time in the high school I went to as a kid, and she certainly had a sense that things were not what they once were. Even in the rural South things were getting out of hand, and my mother had gotten out before it got too bad. I asked her why she had wanted to be a teacher in the first place: it was her teacher in elementary school where her father had been the school custodian. After school was over and all the kids went home, my mother stayed behind to help him clean, wiping down her classmates' desks, washing the chalkboards, sweeping the floors. She'd had a reading disability as a young girl, and it embarrassed her to be the only child taken out of the class each day to get the help she needed to improve. Then one day her teacher gave her a book called *Wings for Per.* "I think you'll like this, dear." It was based on a true story of a young boy, living high in the mountains of an unnamed European hamlet, who, upon seeing the eagles flying overhead and out to the sea, dreamed, like all children, of one day being able to fly himself. Then war descends on his country, destroying his mountain paradise. As Per escapes by fishing boat and hides from the enemy in the caves high above his village, he vows to return one day and set his tiny village free.

My mother's teacher was right. She fell in love with Per's story, and with reading. "I can still see the cover now," she told me, as she choked up recalling the book. And even more, from that point on, washing the chalkboards and tidying her classmates' desks after school, my mother imagined that she, too, might one day become a teacher and teach other children to fly. Touched by that memory, I asked her whether she'd ever cut up in school. "I'd better not cut up. My dad was the custodian." That's the boring part. The part where the beautiful symphony hits a sour note at the end, ruining the performance. The part that makes us shift in our seats and feel restless or bored. The uplifting part—the story of how reading liberated my mother and helped her become her greater, more gifted self—is the part we, understandably, prefer to latch onto.

But being an adult citizen of a complex democracy means not

just doing the fun and inspiring parts, but diving hard, and in good faith, into the difficult parts, the boring parts, too, the parts that make us uncomfortable. It is said that politicians campaign in poetry, but govern in prose. Most books that discuss teaching discuss the poetry of it. This book has been mostly about its prose. The only way we can meaningfully enjoy the romantic and emotionally stirring parts is if the grown-ups deal with the less romantic and less emotionally stirring parts too: making sure some semblance of helpful and healthy communal authority is restored to schools.

I talked all this through with my mom over Christmas. It was a serious and grown-up conversation. But none of that changed the fact that come January I would be standing, day in and day out, in front of a roomful of tenth-graders, most of whom couldn't have cared less about the quality of my poetry or my prose.

7

Less Than Zero Tolerance

Ethan Adshade stared in disbelief. The principal of Countee Cullen Charter School was openly cursing at him. Ethan understood that he was a new teacher, but what had he done to deserve this? Fresh out of Teach for America (TFA) training, he'd landed an interview with the school and had spent days preparing. In the middle of his sample teaching—the ten-minute exercise schools require of aspiring teachers to prove they actually know what they're doing—the principal and then the assistant principal started cursing at him. They were, apparently, pretending to be students, but Ethan had not foreseen this. He stopped the lesson cold. "This isn't fair," he told them. "If a student curses at me while I'm teaching, I'm going through the disciplinary process."

How they must have pitied him.

The son of a mother who worked as an office assistant and a father who cut down trees for a living, Ethan had been born in Jacksonville, Florida, walking distance from the ocean. His parents divorced when he was born, and by the time he graduated from high school he had become the middle child of a brood of seven full, step-, and half-siblings. His father had been born and raised in a devout Christian home in South Africa, the type of man who would rise from his bed at 3:00 a.m. and drop to his knees, moved by the Holy Spirit to pray. With his conservative working-class roots, Ethan had no plans for college. He wanted to be a firefighter and spend his free time and vacations surfing the Florida coast. But he was in love with a young woman headed to the University of Florida. So during his senior year he filled out a single college application, won admission, and enrolled in U of F to follow his heart. Two weeks after he arrived on campus, his girlfriend broke up with him.

As he stood at the whiteboard ready to demonstrate his teaching ability as a freshly minted high school teacher, his heart was only partly in it. TFA had been merely a stop on his way to much bigger things, to the type of glamorous life he envisioned for himself. Teaching wouldn't get him there. But a degree from Harvard Business School could. So his plan was to do a two-year stint working in an inner-city school to make him appear to be a little more interesting than the status-seeking free-marketer he was at heart. After Harvard, he'd be within reach of the job of his dreams: a high-octane commodities trader at Glencore International, a multinational commodity-trading and mining firm headquartered in Switzerland. The company sounds like something out of an international tech thriller, replete with sleek modern offices in the Netherlands and France as well as Switzerland. He was smitten. No, Ethan never wanted to be a teacher. He wanted to be a shark. But a year at Cullen would change the trajectory of his life.

A week after his teaching tryout, Cullen offered him the job. And on his first day, as he entered the first floor of Cullen's campus, he heard Renata before he saw her. A fifteen-year-old Latina not much more than five feet tall was having a meltdown, screaming at the top of her lungs. Four guards surrounded her and were trying to calm her as she cursed the administrators (two white women and a white man), who walked right past her, into their office, and closed the doors behind them. Ethan tried not to stare as he made his way to the stairs and headed up to the third floor of the still nearly empty school. He entered his classroom and shut the door. *Is this a movie?* he thought to himself. It wasn't. But the kids, some of whom were by now waiting outside his door, had seen the same film he had.

As they entered, he greeted them one by one. Many spoke, others didn't. With his *Grey's Anatomy* good looks and a casual slouch that made his six-foot frame seem a good two inches shorter, the girls (and one or two of the boys) eyed him more than a bit suggestively. One in the pack told him, "Oooh, mister, you got a girlfriend? 'Cuz I want to be that." To this band of kids the teacher appeared to be a stereotypical and seemingly easily bullied figure. He introduced himself and began to call roll; when he came to the name of Francisco Barragan, whom all the kids called Fats, the boy slammed his hand on the desk and delivered the trite but menacing warning: "You ain't in Kansas anymore, white boy. This the ghetto." Yes, Fats and Ethan had seen the same movie. Ethan put on his best teacher voice: "One, we're not going to talk like that in this class. Two, this is not the ghetto; it's Watts, a beautiful and vibrant neighborhood. And three, I've never been to Kansas." A few of the kids laughed. Others just stared. Ethan pressed on through the list of names. Suddenly the door flew open, and a six-foot-four student built like a tank—easily two hundred pounds—walked in. He was wearing one red shoe, like the Blood he was. Without so much as nodding in the teacher's direction, Percy went around the room, pointing to each of the other students in the class and saying to them in turn, "Fuck you, fuck you, you a bitch, I'll kick your ass, you can suck my dick, you alright, fuck you . . ."

Around the room he went, gradually working his way toward Ethan. Percy would be his first big test of the day and he hadn't even finished calling the roll. After his teaching tryout, when the principal and assistant principal cursed him, he'd drawn a line in the sand. He would not let a student get away with cursing at him. He'd have zero tolerance for that. They might fight and curse and disrespect each other, but no one would curse at him directly and get away with it. He was the teacher and that was his boundary. But now the biggest and toughest kid, a bona fide Blood (although Ethan didn't know that at the time), was going around the class and cursing all the kids to their faces without even acknowledging Ethan. Percy was steadily moving toward an empty chair right at the front of the class, a few feet from where Ethan was standing. This kid knew exactly what he was doing and Ethan sensed it. With each curse Percy flung that went unchallenged— by Ethan or the kids—the monopoly of power over the classroom passed more and more securely into Percy's hands. He sent his final bristling rebuke to his classmate ("and yo mamma a bitch too"), then headed straight to the front. Percy stopped feet from him, looked Ethan square in the face, and declared, "*And* I'm gonna get the best grade in the class. Now what *you* got to say?"

Ethan blinked for a few beats. "What's your name?"

"Percy."

Ethan scanned the roster and checked Percy's name off.

"Thank you, Percy. You can have a seat." And Percy did. Test passed. In Ethan's class, Percy would turn out to be a gem.

There would be a thousand other tests that year, and frankly, Ethan would fail plenty of them. But through it all, he maintained a hard-and-fast rule: no cursing at him allowed. The year he arrived at Cullen, a few years after me, his time there would largely mirror mine, except in two important ways: He was bound there for two difficult years; I was a sub and could quit at any time.*

---

* Teach for America is a non-profit organization, founded in 1990, that hires college graduates for two-year stints to teach in America's charter schools.

And despite the exhausting brutality of teaching there, he managed to work a miracle. But like me, he bristled at the sound of young people cursing and was outraged at the idea of a student's cursing at him. He had no tolerance for it.

But what about that phrase, *zero tolerance*? The school policy that drew strict behavioral lines and was a leftover from a previous generation? I saw nothing approaching zero tolerance in the more than fifty schools where I taught during my year as a sub. Or in the more than fifty schools I've been inside since starting to write this book several years ago. Instead I saw the extreme opposite, with teachers and administrators tolerating all manner of bad behavior just to keep kids in school between 8:00 a.m. and 3:00 p.m. And it wasn't just in Los Angeles. A childhood friend who has taught in Miami-Dade County for almost twenty years wrote this to me: "They dismantled the discipline system . . . It is virtually impossible to discipline a student. . . . students are rarely, if ever, suspended. I know we are losing a generation of kids of color as a result of allowing them to run wild." Zero tolerance doesn't exist in Miami-Dade either. So where did it go? Where did it come from? What were its effects on chaotic schools and why had it fallen into such disfavor among education activists?

By now you may be able to guess what sparked the rise of zero tolerance: the same thing that had so upended schools in the first place: the crack trade that hit the major cities in the mid-1980s and by the mid-1990s had radically changed inner-city life. The gangs that until then had been mostly small-time protection rackets had morphed into multimillion-dollar business enterprises that trafficked in one of the most lethal and addictive substances the country had ever seen. And the gang warfare and violence that accompanied it spilled right into the schools.

A survey of California public schools taken in 1994 underscored the unsettling new reality. Nearly 60 percent of students reported seeing someone at school with a weapon. Nearly 40 percent of ninth-graders reported being in a physical fight. Eighteen percent of ninth-graders and 16 percent of eleventh-graders reported that they belonged to a gang.[1] Kids were awash in violence. That these numbers, which matched national trends, covered the entire state and every income level suggests they would well have been higher if the study had counted only schools like Cullen in the poorest inner-city areas.

Zero tolerance was the federal response. Among its advocates was someone many would regard as an unlikely champion: Eric Holder, the man who would become the first black U.S. attorney general under President Barack Obama and who served as Janet Reno's deputy attorney general during the Clinton administration. Today school shootings are so commonplace (more than a dozen in just the first few months of 2018) that we forget how rare gun violence in public schools was to a different generation. "We weren't talking about kids doing routine kinds of bad things in schools," Holder says now. "These were kids with guns who were murdering other kids. There was a real concern that we were losing control as a society."[2] (It is also worth noting that gun violence is largely absent from inner-city schools today in large part as a result of the metal detectors and spot checks put in place to keep vengeful kids from terrorizing their classmates with guns.)

In 1994 Congress enacted the Gun-Free Schools Act, which denies federal funds to states if they have failed to pass legislation cracking down on guns and gangs in schools. The law mandated immediate expulsion of any student who brought a gun to school. The crackdown was immediate and transformed some schools overnight. Students and parents alike largely approved of the policy. Who could oppose expelling students who brought a gun to school? How could that be wrong? Opposition did materialize, and eventually the unhelpful, unintended consequences of the law made the problem worse, even as it became clear that in 1994 the federal government had been playing catch-up.

Nearly a decade earlier a telegenic and forceful advocate had calmed the nation's legitimate fears and captured the nation's imagination. He's been long forgotten, but he was once a giant in education. His name was Joe Clark.

Clark, a forty-five-year-old African American, was a former teacher who had become principal of one of New Jersey's toughest schools, Eastside High, in the failing old industrial city of Paterson in the northern part of the state. The school had become for many a glaring symbol of the deteriorating public school system, riddled with drugs and violence. Clark had emerged as something of a turnaround artist after taking over a low-performing New Jersey middle school and dramatically improving student test scores within a few short years. The superintendent of New Jersey schools had tapped Clark to duplicate that success at Eastside. With his hard-line policies and flair for the dramatic, Clark began to attract media attention. He once bolted shut the front doors of the school to keep the drug dealers out. As his law-and-order reputation spread at the height of the 1980s drug epidemic—he had zero tolerance for even the tiniest infractions—Clark managed to drive the gangs and guns from the school. His success, along with his bluster and charisma, led to profiles of him in national publications in the late 1980s, praise from then president Ronald Reagan, and Clark's photo on the cover of *Time* magazine, which showed him brandishing his trademark baseball bat under the headline "Is Getting Tough the Answer?" Dubbed the "Rambo of public education," Clark became a national hero, played by Morgan Freeman in the 1989 film *Lean on Me*. Four years later, when Holder was making a name for himself in Bill Clinton's Justice Department and was alarmed at the growing violence in the cities, zero tolerance policies became federal law.

Both the feature film and documentary footage of Clark from that time make clear that zero tolerance began as an admirable and well-intentioned policy. The Gun-Free Schools Act required all states that received federal funds to expel students who brought guns to school.

So how did it become controversial? Guns, gangs, and drugs were in a tight orbit in the late 1980s and early 1990s. Where one was, the others would inevitably appear. But banning guns in schools, as zero tolerance statutes required, didn't stop violence, because gang members simply brought knives to school instead. So then the schools banned all weapons under zero tolerance. But that didn't stop brutal fights, because brass knuckles could crack a jaw or lacerate an eye. So administrators also issued stringent punishments to anyone carrying brass knuckles. A Justice Department report tracks this expansion: "Many States and communities have expanded on GFSA [Gun-Free Schools Act] and created policies of zero tolerance for all weapons, including toys."[3] But even if schools managed to banish weapons from their halls, the motives behind the violence—gang rivalries, drug money—remained. The next step was to ban anything that signified drugs and gangs in the name of making schools safer. This was the public school version of mission creep. Wearing gang colors, huddling in bathrooms during passing periods, and selling things without permission from the administration—chips, candy—while hoarding wads of cash, considered contraband, all fell under the suspicious eye of punitive administrators trying to drive violence out of the toughest schools.

This process is visible in early footage of Clark, who initiated his own crackdown while New Jersey jurisdictions enacted local zero tolerance policies even before Congress did. In one news clip from the late 1980s, Clark can be heard telling a student at Eastside, "In the hallway without a pass? Automatic suspension."[4] *Why was this kid in the hall without a pass?* Clark must have thought. *He knows the rules. He either walked out of class without permission or is avoiding going to class. Why?* As principals around the country began to follow Clark's charismatic lead, the unforgiving new approach grew to include petty infractions that might once have been handled with a rebuke or tongue lashing. Suspensions and expulsions soared.

But students felt safer. A *New York Times* story from 1999 quotes a black student as saying, "I feel safer at school than I do at home." The real-time footage of Joe Clark shows him at a lectern addressing a school assembly of all black students and proclaiming, "I'm gonna carry this bat and any drug pusher I see trying to enter those 35 doors, I'm going to beat the hell out of him."[5] The auditorium erupts in a rapturous ovation.

I had my own experience in this violent era when I was twelve and left my rural hometown to stay with my cousins for the summer on Chicago's South Side, the first time I was away from home without my parents. Within a few weeks I watched a man across from my aunt's house pull a gun on a couple and open fire as they took off running down the street. At an adult cousin's house I saw a neighbor beat a mentally disabled family friend over the head with a massive four-foot decorative glass bottle until the man collapsed in seizures on the street. On a visit to my great aunt's house, my cousins and I heard a woman down the block screaming at the top of her lungs. Once the ambulance left, we went to her apartment building and saw blood covering the concrete floor of the entryway, where someone had stabbed her repeatedly. I can still see the toilet paper someone had strewn in a vain attempt to absorb the blood. Only tiny flecks of white remained because the blood had soaked completely through it. When my parents called to talk with me at the end of my second week away, I went into my aunt's bedroom so my cousins wouldn't hear me and begged my parents, through tears, to let me come home. If some version of this type of violence was spilling into public schools in large cities (and it was), who can object when politicians and school administrators, urged by parents, students, and community leaders, did whatever they could to stop it?

Among the unhelpful consequences was that teachers and principals no longer had disciplinary discretion because they feared they'd be sued for racial discrimination. If a white kid picked a fight with a black kid and the principal sent the white kid home for three days because he had started the fight and the black kid for one day because he was simply defending himself, someone might perceive the decision as race-based discrimination that opened the principal and school district to a lawsuit. The result was that many states and municipalities established a strict set of automatic consequences for a growing variety of offenses that might have once been viewed as commonplace adolescent horseplay.[6] This strict system of school-based crime and punishment was exacerbated by the presence of police on school campuses. As with other aspects of zero tolerance, schools initially brought police to campus to deal strictly with guns. But once weapons and drugs were gone, the laws mandating police involvement in schools remained in place, leaving police to deal with far less serious infractions. And principals, eager to safeguard themselves from lawsuits, happily relinquished responsibility to them. This was why a cop could handcuff and pat down a perfectly innocent and entirely well-behaved seventh-grade student I came to know for selling bags of Doritos (contraband) on campus and hoarding wads of cash. The district rules against contraband required the administration to call the police. In 2015 a video surfaced of a rabidly angry white cop in South Carolina who was pulling a high school student from her seat and tackling her after she first refused to put away her phone during class and then ignored repeated requests by the teacher and the principal to give them her phone. Finally she had refused to leave the class with the principal. The cop's reaction was a classic example of how outdated policies that placed police on campuses, recalcitrant students, and aggressive, poorly trained police officers could lead to frightening outcomes way out of proportion to the offense. The subsequent revelation that the child had grown up in foster homes provides us with a stronger sense of how an unparented child who'd not been raised with a healthy respect for "domestic," helpful authority, such as parents and teachers, can lead to confrontations with out-of-control, punitive authority.

The other quite dire consequence of zero tolerance legislation, however, was even worse. The Justice Department itself warned in a 1999 report, "Gun-carrying students can, and should, continue to receive educational services. Alternative education programs for weapon-carrying students are likely to succeed if they contain the following elements: administrators with vision and commitment, extensive contact with motivated and specially trained school staff, needs-based individualized instruction, focused classes with low student-to-staff ratios, innovative presentations of materials related to real life, caring and supportive environments, intensive counseling for students and their families, and frequent student progress reports."[7]

To read this now is to see just how humane the federal actors behind zero tolerance like Eric Holder were. It reads like a blueprint for setting up charter schools. The problem was that the federal government provided no funds for establishing these alternative schools. The 1994 federal law required that students be expelled but gave states no resources for educating them. Reform schools and juvenile halls were suddenly packed to the rafters. Consequently, students wound up unsupervised and at home, which is to say on the streets, where they would inevitably fall behind academically and into even more trouble.

The notorious "school-to-prison" pipeline emerged from all these failures to think through the consequences of zero tolerance. All these—automatic punishments for once-minor offenses, police involvement in routine behavioral problems, expulsions that left unsupervised students to roam the streets—were the result of establishing draconian consequences to replace more thoughtful methods of correcting behavior.

* * *

We can all agree that a reexamination of a democratic society's laws is (and should be) a necessary part of democratic self-governance. As times change and social mores evolve, updating, altering, and improving the relationship between the citizen and the state ensures a nation's health. But as rival political factions jostle for power and greater glamour attends to younger generations that entirely reject the actions and ideas of older generations, overcorrection is always and everywhere a risk. "Every generation overturns the work of its predecessor," Rousseau says in *Emile*.[8] If it is true that racism at one point kept great writers like Toni Morrison and Zora Neale Hurston out of the canon, the thing to do is to say there is no such thing as a canon, that quality is a social construct designed to oppress. Best to chuck the whole thing. Some will say Obama declined to intervene in Syria because Obama overcorrected the ghastly mistake of his predecessor. Some will say Obama's successor is overcorrecting him.

And overcorrection is what we have seen in public education rather than a patient reevaluation of our predecessors. Behavior is as bad as it's ever been and in some instances worse. Weapons are gone (mercifully), but in many schools chaos still reigns. Why? The political faddishness that is a woefully permanent part of public education reform has amped up our instinct to overcorrect, with school districts in large cities like Los Angeles, New York, and Chicago, suddenly and without much warning, outlawing suspensions altogether and making expulsions nearly impossible, no matter the offense. As I indicated in chapter 3, when suspensions are gone, detention is meaningless because the consequence for skipping detention no longer exists. And the ban on suspensions means parents are off the hook because they no longer have to deal with a kid who's been sent home for the day for starting a fight or being disrespectful, thus, weakening parental accountability. You must know, too, that this is not a secret. Kids are abundantly aware that they can no longer be suspended, that there is no detention or any real consequence for their behavior, unless it is criminally extreme. Two middle school girls, whom I told to leave my class and go to the office for being disrespectful to me, openly refused to leave. At the age of thirteen, they literally said no, they weren't going anywhere. I called the campus aide and they refused him too. Finally, after ten minutes of wrangling with them, one got up and said, "C'mon, let's go. You know nothing's gonna happen to us anyway." And they were absolutely right.

The Los Angeles Unified School District (LAUSD) now monitors how many students its principals suspend, as the district proudly touts the (forced) decline in suspension numbers, insisting the radically new methods of dealing with misbehavior have worked miracles. It is a regrettable hoax. One of the most shocking experiences I had during my time as a substitute was reading an article about a school in the LAUSD in an online journal, *NationSwell*, "Suspending Students Isn't Effective. Here's What Schools Should Do Instead." The underline claimed that the school had "discovered that getting rid of the disciplinary action actually improves pupil behavior." According to the article, "Led by a new principal and funded by a federal grant . . . an inner-city junior high school . . . joined the growing movement of implementing restorative justice in schools: Instead of simply penalizing misbehavior, the strategy involves talking through the reasons why a child is acting out. Prioritizing resolution over retribution, the school has taken the idea to a whole new level. Last school year, out of 827 middle school students, only 13 were booted from class—an astonishing 98.9 percent drop from 10 years ago." The report went on to describe a student who pulled a fire alarm at the end of the school day and then appeared the next morning in the principal's office. "'I just wanna know,'" the child is reported to have said. "'If I can have a cup of hot chocolate and explain what happened? Before you hear it from anyone else.' 'Who does that?' the principal responded with affectionate awe."[9]

When I came across that article while I was writing this book, my jaw dropped. I had worked at the school during the period the article was describing. It was a madhouse. The article mentioned the one student who confessed to pulling a fire alarm but made no mention of the ten other times someone pulled the fire alarm in the course of a few days or the actual fire that was set in a trash can, filling the halls with smoke and shutting the school down for the day. It made no mention of the four teachers assaulted by students or the vice principal who was punched in the face. It made no mention of the dozen fights that erupted at the same time one day. It also made no mention of why only thirteen students were booted from classes: because the principal forbade teachers from doing so, not because violence and chaotic behavior were any less frequent or severe but simply so she could report that no one was booted from class. In all these incidents but one, none of the students were suspended.

If you doubt the veracity of my experience of what a school turns into when zero tolerance has been overcorrected, a story in the *Los Angeles Times* outlines a similarly difficult experience: "At Los Angeles Academy Middle School in South L.A. [the school where I found a student with a crack rock in my class], teachers . . . are overwhelmed by what they consider ineffective responses to students who push, threaten and curse them. The stress over discipline prompted two teachers to take leaves of absence in the last two months . . . Many teachers felt that administrators were pushing the burden of discipline onto instructors because they can no longer suspend unruly students and lack the staff to handle them outside the classroom." The paper quoted the school union rep as saying, "My teachers are at their breaking point. Everyone working here is highly aware of how the lack of consequences has affected the site. Teachers . . . are walking a fine line between extreme stress and an emotional meltdown."[10] A teacher in Chicago, where suspensions were also banned, was quoted as saying, "It's just basically been a totally lawless few months."[11] Teachers from New York to Chicago echoed these sentiments about the ban on suspensions.[12]

When LAUSD announced it was banning suspensions, the then superintendent proclaimed an end to "early criminalization."[13] So what has been the result of the ban? The *Los Angeles Times* quoted a cop saying that schools were increasingly relying on the police to handle disruptive students. "Now that they can't suspend, schools want to have officers handle things."[14] So the overcorrection that was supposed to curtail the "criminalization" of students and limit their contact with police was actually having the opposite effect and increasing it. But, of course it would. I know a single father who was told by the Department of Children and Family Services (DCFS) that not only could he not spank his outrageously behaved pre-teen daughter, who'd called DCFS on him, but he couldn't even make her do push-ups because that was corporal punishment and against the law. Desperate for help, he asked them what he could do. Their answer? Call the police on her. So the police had been to his home half a dozen times to deal with his unruly adolescent, a sight that sickened him every time their black-and-white cruisers pulled into his driveway to quell behavior parents have been responsibly correcting since time immemorial. When healthy "domestic" forms of stringency from parents and teachers are eviscerated by ridiculous rule-makers, the only forms left are the "foreign," punitive ones, and those people are always armed with guns. This is what black parents have always meant when they say, "We better get them, before the police do."

The chasing of fads, of being the first to innovate or correct or disrupt the supposedly antiquated habits of the past, is one of the most massive and critical failures of modern education reform. Education advocates who scream that zero tolerance is destroying schools have no knowledge of the world they're describing. And rather than undertaking a careful look at the Gun-Free Schools Act, which had serious positive consequences, to see what went wrong (lack of quality alternative schools for the suspended and expelled), school districts rush to overcorrect. The *Los Angeles Times* article described the LAUSD this way: "Hailed by the White House and others for its *leadership* in promoting more progressive school-discipline policies . . . the nation's second-largest school system was the *first* in California to ban suspensions for defiance."[15] School boards crave such empty praise. With their addiction to innovation—to be the most politically and educationally progressive actors in the public school marketplace, with no concern for common sense or the intellectual rigor that characterizes other academic fields—the politically motivated purveyors of American education reform reject the most basic tools of education—patient investigation, patient questioning, patient response. Instead, every few years they dream up new ways and means and then force the largely powerless students and parents to yield to the demands of the reformers' newfangled conceptual toy. Unraveling what became of zero tolerance put me as close as I'd been so far to solving the still-central mystery of why chaos had been given such free rein in public schools, though I knew undiscovered answers were still out there somewhere.

As for Ethan Adshade, he held the line at cursing him, so much so that when kids wanted to get kicked out of class, to meet up with friends, hang out in the bathroom, or chill in the main office, all they had to do was call him a "fucking bitch" and out they went. He never quite figured out a way to bend the rule so that they wouldn't win. Occasionally he'd say, "Naw, you're just trying to get kicked out, so you're staying right here," but then other hellishness would ensue. And at the end of the day, it was better to let a kid leave if she didn't want to be in class than force her to stay. As for Percy, Ethan never had trouble with him. For whatever reason

8

Follow the Money

The new year brought with it the thin, cold rain of a Los Angeles winter. It also brought with it answers to a mystery: why the trouble that started with the crack epidemic had been allowed to last so long. I came back to Los Angeles three days before the start of the new semester at Cullen. I was petrified. I had been told that lesson plans would be left for me but I should feel free "to expand on them" if I wanted to. It felt like I'd been told to shoot myself. What did I know about expanding lesson plans? I'd had a talk with the English teacher who was primarily responsible for helping the handful of seniors who had not yet passed the California High School Exit Examination (CAHSEE) do so. I'd have a class just for them, no more than five or six students. I knew a few of the students, and with one exception they were well behaved and desperately wanted that diploma. The CAHSEE was not easy, and trying to make students literate enough in English and reading comprehension in a few months would be tough. Luckily, that wasn't my sole or even primary responsibility. The teacher had taught lessons she wanted me to reinforce and I agreed, but I told her I'd focus on vocabulary. I'd seen a sample test that asked for definitions of at least five or six words with no context provided. I wanted to be sure the students missed none of those words and would be able to parse or recognize the vocabulary in the reading passages. The goal was a modest but serious one. And five to ten guaranteed points is a lot when you're facing the prospect of not graduating.

The day before my first day teaching full time, I was lying in bed when I realized my nerves were fried. I was worried not only about helping those few seniors pass the CAHSEE but about the general crop of kids I'd be dealing with. Just about every class held some potential for trouble, but each included lots of gems and plenty of funny, charming, or, at worst, aggravating knuckleheads. *I'll focus on them*, I thought, as I ran through the names and faces of the kids I sensed I could rely on or could win over. I'd have Dayshawn and Greg, but not Demetrius (he'd dropped out by then) or David. No Junior, but Rodiney and Clarice. And I'd also, in my sixth period class, have Erik.

One day shortly before the bell rang about a week after I started full time, I saw Erik leaving a first-year teacher's class, cursing a blue streak. Fuck this. Bitch-ass that. The teacher was a young black guy from the South and fresh out of Teach for America training, not more than twenty-two years old, but looking all of seventeen and whippet thin. As Erik exited, I peered into the teacher's room and saw that he was pretty rattled. I tried to encourage him and tell him he was hardly the only one. That this kid was a hellion and no one seemed prepared to help teachers deal with him. The problem with Erik was the air of unpredictability and the eye for vulnerability he seemed to have. He had a preternatural sense of who to bully. He knew teachers really wouldn't curse back at him (one or two did, but they were chastised by the administration), certainly not new ones, or have any interest in fighting him. There were stronger, tougher guys at Cullen who could have laid out Erik with a single blow, but they had self-control and didn't get into random fights. For my part, I'd already mentioned to Mr. Titus that if Erik was in my class, I was going to need support. There was only one counselor in the school, and he seemed ineffective. I wasn't fighting with that kid all day; I was only going to deal with being called a bitch ass so many times. I'd be sending Erik out every day he talked crazy to me. Mr. Titus said he understood. His hands were tied with Erik because the principal (a white woman, younger than Titus, who was in her first year as principal) seemed scared of him. I knew I could make it work as long as Titus backed me. But the new semester threw a wrench in my plans; there was a new assistant principal for ninth and tenth grade, and I'd be answering to him, not Titus. Who knew what this new guy's theory of classroom behavior was? (And they always have a theory.) It would be just my luck if he were one of the hardcore we-don't-send-kids-to-the-office administrators.

After a word of encouragement to the new teacher about Erik, I turned back into the hall to get to my class before the bell rang. I saw a parent in the hall who'd overheard Erik on his rant. She looked in my direction and said, mostly to herself, "That's what fifty dollars a day will get you," and continued on down the hall. In that instant, I had the same jolt of revelation I'd had when I'd heard Jay-Z on the radio saying crack had destroyed communal authority. Her comment rang in my head as the answer to a question that I had been hunting for. I hadn't the faintest idea what she was talking about, but it was like the outlines of a door, one that I never knew was there, appeared in my brain. Finding the key to unlock it and sort through the secrets beyond it would take strenuous effort, but at least now, at last, I knew the door was there.

I'd discover that all our most urgent questions about race, class, and opportunity can be boiled down to that stray comment in the hall of Countee Cullen Charter High School. The mother was saying quite a bit. But I didn't figure out the answer to the riddle until I encountered the story of a woman in Idaho named Anne Markham. At the start of flu season in Idaho some years ago, her son's charter school had sent a letter home saying that parents should send their children to school even if they were feeling sick. Markham was perplexed. Didn't everyone know that flu was most contagious in its early stages, when kids were feeling just a little sick? What school wants its classrooms full of sniffling, aching, runny-nosed, possibly flu-ridden kids? Was not missing a day of algebra that crucial? The lawyer in her was sure something else was going on.

Many public schools in the United States, especially in places where charter schools abound, receive funding according to the number of students who attend classes. That is, the money flows only if a child is marked present.* So these schools do whatever they have to do to make sure students are there each day.

This bizarre arrangement has bred trouble, including encouraging schools to keep outrageous students like Erik under their roof, no matter how much trouble they cause. But that's only part of the problem. My year of subbing at dozens of charter and traditional public schools, as well as private and parochial ones, made clear to me that, against every instinct we might have as Americans who cherish the notion of social mobility and free-market competition, money and choice—the modern-day payment by results— have emerged as the biggest obstacles to educating poor and disadvantaged youth.

The idea of school choice began in 1955 when the famed economist Milton Friedman proposed the use of school vouchers to allow parents to purchase tuition for any school, private, public, or religious. Designed as a kind of educational traveler's check, the vouchers would be given to parents directly by the state. This would mean parents were not bound to their local school, and, according to Friedman,

---

* This policy was initially designed to curb truancy. The deleterious effects of this approach to funding schools have been exacerbated by the competition from charters for student enrollment.

the competition to secure the parents' money would spur innovation at, and improvement of, the schools. This belief has become gospel in U.S. society, so much so that nearly sixty-five years later, a wealthy patron parroted this reasoning almost verbatim while explaining his million-dollar donation to Yale: "Private funding makes for a more competitive environment, where schools have to compete for funding, faculty, students, and reputation, and that fosters free-market competition, which makes things great here." It's nonsense. If Friedman and the patron are right, our nation's K–12 private schools would be proof of the viability of his proposal, but the only comprehensive comparative study found that, on the whole, students who'd gone to state-funded public schools outperformed students who had gone to private schools (and charter schools too).[1] Why? Because competition and capitalism tends to eviscerate school standards; it doesn't raise them. Harvard offers perhaps the best example of this dynamic.

A doctoral candidate in classics at Harvard had taught a tiny third-year Latin course there; her grading rubric was clearly spelled out in her syllabus at the start of the semester. At the end of a demanding term, she gave out only one A. After she submitted her grades, she was summoned to meet with the professor overseeing the course; waiting for her was an angry student who'd received an A–. The student had wanted an A because, he said, he'd "worked really hard." The professor apparently agreed and, without ever asking to see the student's work or the course's grading rubric, simply pressed the (untenured) lecturer to admit that she had made a mistake in assessing the quality of the disgruntled student's work. The headline on her op-ed piece was "How Harvard Helps Its Richest and Most Arrogant Students Get Ahead."[2] Because the student was seen as a "potential friend of the department" (donor), the rules were readily bent to satisfy his demand. Make a school a business that depends directly on its customers for funding, and the wealthy will get the grades they seek.

(This story was especially gratifying to me. When I was an undergrad in Cambridge, a famous conservative professor blamed grade inflation on the arrival of black students and the unwillingness of liberal professors to assess them accurately. The professor offered no proof and never mentioned the role of money in warping admissions and grading standards at the most prestigious school in the world. Jared Kushner, anyone?)

My personal experience teaching in private schools bore out what happened at Harvard. Some years after my year as a substitute, I took on brief part-time work in private schools (partly as research for this book). Within my first few days at a school, the academic director, who was in charge of teacher evaluations and had hiring and firing power, said to me, "Our students are all pretty much B students." This was not true. Not even close. There were B students, A students, and plenty of C students, and a solid share of students who deserved F's, but the message was clear to me (and other teachers): I never gave out anything lower than a C, and even those were extremely rare. In fact, it was openly discussed among staff that kids weren't being given grades they truly deserved because the paying parents, on whom the school depended to keep its doors open, would complain. About one kid in particular, whose work in my class was very poor, I was warned that if I gave him anything less than an A, I (and the principal) would hear from his mother, who was on the school's board of directors. Another student who did no work at all in my class for the entire year, and who would have easily gotten an F in public school, ended up receiving a C because his mother complained angrily to the principal, who thought it best that the student's future not be "too sorely impacted."

The wealthy parents of underperforming children do not tolerate your giving their cherubs D's or F's, even when they abundantly deserve them. Then, if you do, those wealthy parents will simply threaten to pull all of their children out of the offending school and find another one that will welcome their sixty, ninety, or one hundred twenty thousand dollars a year. In other words, when parents control the financial health of a school, the product is no longer a public good (as economists refer to them) but a private individual good, like a pair of shoes or a Maserati, and that product is no longer the quality of the education, but the quality of the grade.

Some further proof of the effect private money and institutions can have on standards: Perhaps the most famous privately created secondary educational institution is the International Baccalaureate, also known as the IB, invented in Switzerland in 1968. It now exists in many public schools in the United States but was first created as a way to provide continuity and rigor to the education of the world's roving diplomatic elite. It can be a rigorous and demanding curriculum, but the grading rubric, which is set by an international private body, can make it difficult to assess a child's true achievement. I provide here actual grades from a single teacher in a private school in New York. Bear in mind that the grading scale for IB classes is based on a seven-point international scale, which, for American students, is then translated into a letter grade.

History IB SL 11
Teacher: **LEVINE, Brian**
Grade Scale:
1-7 IB History/Physics/Music Scale
10Intl-12IB
S2 Grade: **5 A–**

History IB SL 11
Teacher: **LEVINE, Brian**
Grade Scale:
1-7 IB History/Physics/Music Scale
10Intl-12IB
S2 Grade: **6 A**

History IB SL 11
Teacher: **LEVINE, Brian**
Grade Scale:
1-7 IB History/Physics/Music Scale
10Intl-12IB
S2 Grade: **6 A+**

History IB SL 11
Teacher: **LEVINE, Brian**
Grade Scale:
1-7 IB History/Physics/Music Scale
10Intl-12IB
S2 Grade: **7 A+**

Four different students received 5's, 6's, and 7's on a seven-point scale, but they all got A's.

But how does this relate to public schools? Choice and competition mean that public schools are now every bit as desperate to secure the $9,500 they get in public funds for each student every year (in California) as expensive private schools are to secure the money they get from rich parents. And because states, from California to Utah, where competition from charters is sharp, typically calculate the money according to the number of students who attend each day, administrators are willing to do just about anything to make sure that once a parent chooses their school, they stick with it and that the kid is marked present every single day. That includes insisting that sick students come to school during flu season or refusing to suspend an aggressive and out-of-control kid for threatening a teacher. This is what economists call perverse incentives—when the money you receive to solve a problem has consequences that make the problem even worse.

And grade inflation in traditional public schools has become as bad as ever because it allows them to compete with charter schools.

The charters are governed by different rules than traditional public schools and thus have an unfair advantage (more on that shortly). The response of traditional public schools has been to make graduation easier and easier so they can pretend that their students are thriving just like the ones in charter schools are said to be (albeit mistakenly). It is perfectly commonplace to turn on the radio in Los Angeles and hear the head of the local school district saying, "Our graduation rates are better than they've ever been." I always want to ask, "Yeah, they're graduating, but can they read and write?" This is not an idle question. In 2013 the *Los Angeles Times* wrote about a freshman at UC Berkeley who'd graduated with straight A's from a traditional high school in South Los Angeles and was his class's salutatorian. Now he was on the verge of flunking out of college because he couldn't write an intelligible five-paragraph essay.

> It was early January, and he stared nervously at his first college transcript. There wasn't much good to see. He had barely passed an introductory science course. In College Writing 1A, his essays— pockmarked with misplaced words and odd phrases—were so weak that he would have to take the class again. He had never felt this kind of failure, nor felt this insecure. The second term was just days away and he had a 1.7 GPA. If he didn't improve his grades by school year's end, he would flunk out.[3]

I hate quoting this story in part because conservative opponents of worthwhile affirmative action will use it to bolster their generally nonsensical fantasies, but such a lack of preparedness is wholly unprecedented and due, in no small part, to the modern world of free-market choice. (I object to grade inflation because it means that no one identifies a student's weaknesses before he winds up at UC Berkeley incapable of crafting a sentence.)

Although social promotion has long been a part of public and private schools, it rarely seeped into the highest levels of achievement. An A earned in Honors English classes at my predominantly black school in a rural town in the South was as hard earned an A as one at a competitive private school in New Hampshire. The public school system in my town of fewer than four thousand people sent me to Harvard, my sister to Duke and Yale, and classmates to the Air Force Academy and Vanderbilt as well as other top-tier colleges across the country. And each of us thrived. And, more important, our predominantly black high school was the only game in town. It didn't have to pretend kids were thriving when they weren't because their parents would enroll them in the rival school across the street, where the administration was handing out diplomas like Pez candies and graduation rates were "higher." Both schools were funded with single-line items based on average enrollment; while this system surely has its weaknesses (which should be addressed), it remains the only guarantor of equality and fairness, the only guarantor that schools aren't bullied by a parent threatening to remove their child because Timmy didn't pass algebra. It's the only guarantor that an A+ means something qualitatively different from an B.

The most recent numbers show that charters have brought no substantial improvement in student performance. Even supporters of the charter school movement acknowledge they have been far from a panacea. In addition to the study I mentioned above showing students in public schools doing better than students in private ones, it also showed traditional public schools were superior to charters. The well-known documentary *Waiting for Superman* also publicized a study that showed a third of students in charters perform at the same level as their counterparts in traditional public schools, a third do not perform as well, and a third perform better.[4] A more recent study showed even weaker results, with 56 percent showing no improvement over traditional schools, roughly 20 percent showing improvement, and 20 percent doing more poorly. It also showed that states that shut down their lowest-performing charter schools fared better overall.[5]

But what of the students in charter schools who outperform their counterparts in traditional schools? Let me tell you about one of them. As I was finishing this book, I once again became a sub because I was curious to see how things had or hadn't changed in the more than five years since I'd decided to write it. I was assigned to a remarkable charter school in the Westlake neighborhood of Los Angeles. I'll call the school Westmont. The demographic breakdown of its students was 55 percent white or Asian, 30 percent Latino, 5 percent black, and 8 percent mixed. These numbers are impressively diverse until you look at the demographics of the area. Westlake is 5.9 percent white, 17.5 percent Asian, 71 percent Latino, and 4.6 percent black. According to census data, "the median household income was roughly $29,000, a low figure for Los Angeles, and a high percentage of households earned $20,000 or less." But perhaps more interesting is that nearly 70 percent of the residents of Westlake were born abroad. The main countries of their birth were Mexico and El Salvador, yet only 7 percent of Westmunt students needed help with English.[6]

Needless to say, although the charter school boasts of retaining a "neighborhood feel," it did not draw any significant numbers from the poor Latino, non-English-speaking population around it. (The last time I subbed there for an eighth-grade class, there were twenty students, fourteen of whom were white; one fully black; three Asian; and two, to my eye, biracial. Not at all similar to the make-up of the local neighborhood.) In fact, I already knew one student at the school because I'd taught him briefly at a private school I'd worked at part time a few years after I subbed. He is white and the private school's tuition was $20,000, nearly equal to the median yearly income of local Westlake residents. He lived nowhere near the school. So how did he get in? Presumably, his name was drawn in a lottery; according to the school's website, this is the only way kids are admitted. The school does not advertise its presence to the local neighborhood nor does it provide detailed information about the lottery process. It does say that weighted preference is given to students in the following categories: siblings of currently enrolled students, children of faculty and staff, children of board members (there were twenty, nearly all white and wealthy), children of founding parents, students zoned to that area, and students eligible for the school lunch program.

This strikes me as a rigged system, one traditional public schools have no chance of replicating. By having a lottery to which parents must apply, the charter school is already guaranteeing it will attract students with a conscientious parent who will track down an unadvertised school not located in their immediate area, fill out the online application, and hope their child is selected. That's not a random pool of parents, it's a preselected group of responsible parents, which traditional schools cannot insist on; traditional schools have to take all comers. Further, the school provides no real details about how the preferences are weighted. Do children of (the mostly white and wealthy) board members and siblings of students get more weight than poor kids with no connections to the school? What if you are both a sibling and a child of faculty? Do you get extra points? Westmont is essentially using public funds to function like a private school. No wonder some charter schools are performing well; they've created nearly unsurpassable barriers for kids without conscientious, informed (English-speaking) parents, something traditional schools cannot do.

The *Los Angeles Times* ran a story exposing just these practices in charter schools all over California, detailing how they create huge barriers to entry for poor public students, weeding out students they find undesirable even before meeting them. One such school in Santa Rosa requires that a student and parent must fill out a twenty-page document *before* even being accepted. The student must write five short essays using "complete sentences" on a range of topics, including one about their family (no doubt a way to find out if they are poor immigrants). And the parents have to write seven essays of their own and fill out forms regarding the child's medical history.[7] Charter schools are a boondoggle for the rich, as they use public funds to create private island paradises to keep the unwanted out.

While at the micro-level some individual charters are thriving, charter schools' effects on the school system at the macro-level have been devastating. Years ago I lived in New York with my college roommate, who was from a wealthy, aristocratic family in Mexico. Both of us were going to be in New York after graduation, so we decided to live together, occupying the two bedrooms of a nearly $10,000-a-month marble-floored high-rise apartment on the Upper West Side for which his parents kindly picked up the tab. My roommate had trained as an economist and had taken a job as an analyst for the *United Nations Human Development Reports*. One night I came home late and starving from a job on Wall Street that I abhorred. He had just arrived too and was sitting at the dining room table eating a cheeseburger. I asked him for some. Rational being that he was, he told me about an economic principle that holds that two starving people splitting a hamburger is an inefficient use of resources and that, logically speaking, it was better for one person to be fully sated than have two starving people split the burger with neither feeling full. My hungry and irritated response was to ask about the economic principle that finds me punching him in the face, fattening his lip, grabbing the burger, and leaving him wounded and woefully without the aforementioned burger. No slouch, he said he'd never heard of such a theory and suspected that I was making it up. I told him he was a poor excuse for an economist if he'd never heard of the Busted Lip Theory of Resource Allocation. We went back and forth for a while, and he eventually gave in to my hectoring and shared part of his tiny meal with me. I was grateful, but it turned out that he was right. I was still hungry.

Not until I worked in public schools did I appreciate the full burden of the half-a-hamburger principle. The school choice charter movement has replaced large traditional public schools with dozens of small charter schools all vying for the same limited amount of daily dollars. But it has not fostered the improvement or innovation its advocates claimed it would. It has fostered desperation because now everyone is getting by on just half a hamburger and nearly everyone is starving. And nearly everyone's in the red. An Oregon study comparing the costs of small schools to those of large schools (all noncharters) detailed the "higher costs associated with small schools."[8] But the inherent benefits of the small schools are a sacred part of the charter movement's public relations packet, so no one has really examined the downside of having tons and tons of underfunded small schools.

The economics of that downside are simple enough. All schools have fixed costs—light bills, heating bills, salaries, building maintenance, and lunches don't go away if no students show up or only half the students show up, so the tiniest fluctuation in daily school enrollment because of illness, a family move, dropouts, parental dissatisfaction, and suspensions spells disaster for small schools. (Large schools have the advantage of economies of scale, which spread costs out over a larger population.) But if thirty students in a school population of five hundred located in a tough area have poor attendance (and there are always more than thirty), that's nearly $300,000 gone from a small school's coffers. That easily wipes out six teacher salaries so suddenly that small school is a small school with large classes because they are down six teachers, instantly defeating the purpose of having a small school.

And the loss of teachers is just the beginning. Day in and day out, I went into both charter and traditional public schools that had been stripped to the bone because of the fierce competition for insufficient funding. Schools with no band, no football team, no basketball team, no cheerleaders, no home economics classes, no shop or art class, no gymnasium for PE, no chorus, no school play, no library (or no librarian to run the library if the school had one), no proms, no yearbook, no school newspaper, no computer lab, no student council, no repairs to crumbling infrastructure, no therapists to treat students with emotional problems, no resource specialist to help students who are in fifth grade but still can't read or the eleventh-grader who didn't know he had to capitalize the letter *i* in a first-person essay or how to use a dictionary. No extra campus aides (bull elephants) to deal with the knuckleheads and assholes, no afterschool tutoring. The list goes on.

To go into a massive school in an inner-city neighborhood, packed now with a half-dozen competing charter schools, was to enter an abandoned carapace and imagine the rich world of black and brown students and teachers who once flourished there. The library was stocked with books, but its doors were locked because the school had no librarian. The music stands still ringed the conductor's pit in the orchestra rooms, but the conductor had long since vanished.

In this competitive marketplace the wholesale elimination (and disregard for) extracurricular activities because of small schools' inability to afford them sorely misunderstands their role in the lifeblood of a neighborhood and the development of a child. Sports rivalries bind neighborhoods together, as current students and alumni show up for the annual homecoming game against the crosstown rival. Band and choral concerts give parents, rich and poor, a chance to turn out in their Sunday finest to hear their children play the jazz piece they've practiced for months. Student councils give kids the first taste of what being a citizen means. For kids who fail at traditional academics, co-curricular education (activities that supplement academics) can mean everything: an ability to weld a seam better than anyone gives them a sense of accomplishment; learning to read music trains their ear, helps them learn math, and gives them access to greater forms of artistic pleasure; discovering they have a lovely voice makes children shunned by classmates suddenly seem beautiful. All the elements of democratic citizenry—cooperation, respect for diversity, mutual dependence, the identification of leaders—are on far more dramatic display in the group dynamics of co-curricular activities than they ever could be in a math or English class.

A generation ago my high school in the rural South provided me and my classmates with all these things and French and Latin classes too. From getting the lead in the elementary school play I learned that I could speak well in front of a room of strangers (something I've done regularly as an adult); band class taught me that I had an ear for music and that I could mark time well (I've written about music for major magazines); in chorus I learned I could carry a tune (my knowledge of vocal performance led in part to a documentary about a major musical artist); Field Day competition told me that I could run faster than most kids my age (when the cops chased me and my cousins on the South Side of Chicago, I made it home before everyone else—not every accomplishment is artistic); taking Latin for a year helped me improve my SAT score; and art class taught me that I'd never know how to draw.

The American chef Bobby Flay and the French chef Alexandre Couillon both have recounted how they were utter failures in school, with no direction or future, but that when they walked into a kitchen for the first time and fell under the sway of a great teacher, they suddenly found a calling they didn't know they had. The superstar chef is among the most glamorous new professionals to emerge in recent years, combining science, art, instinct, and experience to produce small masterpieces every day. But the home ec classes, in which a boy who is flunking English could learn he has a flair for cooking, are nowhere to be found in the free market competition version of public schools.

Instead students leave bare-bones charters, and the public

schools whose funds have been siphoned away, without knowing they have any talents, because schools simply can't afford to attempt to train them in anything other than the most rudimentary math and English. School administrators are too busy scrambling to keep the lights on. Perhaps if these tiny and now-threadbare schools, traditional and charter, were churning out math and reading whizzes, we might say good riddance to home ec and shop and band class, but that's far from the case.

But aren't charters an improvement even so? Weren't the traditional schools that existed before school choice genuinely bad? They *were* awful, and no good-faith account of the world charters encountered and sought to replace can deny that. In the introduction I quoted a teacher who'd said his school had always been tough, but the kids used to fight each other, not the teachers; he was describing a chaotic environment in both instances. The crime surge in the aftermath of the Watts riots profoundly changed inner-city Los Angeles. The homicide rate doubled between 1970 and 1979.[9] The schools began to reflect the changing neighborhoods. By the time crack was introduced in 1984 and the crack epidemic peaked in the 1990s, the gang warfare that dominated Los Angeles had entered through the front doors of the city's poorest schools. The charter school movement was thought to be the solution to the schools' social decay but carried as part of its banner the idea that the tenured teachers who'd weathered the changes in their city were agents of that decay. The avatars of the charter school movement arrived ignorant of, or uninterested in, a more thorough look at the world they were entering. Republicans, long eager to dismantle the rights of unions, happily made common cause with progressives enamored of a glamorous but unearned social revolution and joined the assault on the teachers and administrators of our nation's schools.

The charter movement has not been entirely bad. It put the

teaching profession on notice that slipshod and lazy teaching would no longer be tolerated and that old habits and antiquated thinking would be denounced, disrupted, and discarded. It highlighted the potential benefits of small schools when they are properly and responsibly run (that is, not competing with other schools for "clients"): more teacher-student contact, a more closely knit school community, lower dropout rates, a safer environment. And given that, for the first few decades, charters were able to force parents to participate in their child's education by requiring that they volunteer for a handful of hours (a worthwhile demand but one the courts have recently outlawed), they helped provide, at least in theory, a picture of what a successful school might look like, when the "market" was fair and functioning efficiently. Who could quarrel with that?

But like nearly all revolutions, the charter school movement misdiagnosed the disease and exaggerated the cure. What schools needed was not an endless supply of white middle-class recent college grads, barely older than their charges, armed with iPads and the latest in data analytics showing how best to improve reading scores by ten points in a single quarter. What was needed was not a revolving door of untenured teacher after untenured teacher spending a two-year stint in the inner city, championing the forces of "market disruption." These schools did not need free-market disruption but civic-minded stability. Old and antiquated thinking—respect for elders, the inviolate and sacred nature of a school, the importance of stringency as well as sweetness in dealing with undersocialized youth, the civic value of public goods—still had a crucial part to play. These neighborhoods had been disrupted enough, by drugs and violence and militarized policing. No one needed more. Talk to residents of inner-city Los Angeles who came of age before the crime waves and the lost jobs. They speak of the working-class neighborhoods with schools and a civic culture that ably served them. Pockets of violence and social decay were always evident (as were, of course, aggressively racist police), but Countee Cullen High School was once a vibrant and functioning place.

Why, then, do charters remain so popular with the public? Why do so many successful people, from Mark Zuckerberg to P. Diddy, support them? The rich and famous have been drawn to education, largely out of a desire to do good and, perhaps, create a legacy for themselves. (Oprah's opening a school for girls in South Africa ten years ago was a celebrated cultural event and may have inspired other celebrities to do something similar in the United States. But Nelson Mandela had asked Oprah to open a school. She seems to have been suitably and wisely cautious about inserting herself into the public school/charter school debate in the United States.) So the rich and famous can be forgiven this impulse. After all, many wildly successful people are at least partially autodidacts. Mark Zuckerberg spent a year at Harvard, then made himself into the boy-genius founder of Facebook. P. Diddy went to Howard for a year, but Howard didn't make him the music mogul he became. Andre Agassi had great tennis coaches, but he is responsible for his tenacity on the court. So the rich and famous look at failing schools and inevitably think, *I know what it takes to be a success. After all, I created my own, so surely I can figure out what it takes to help other kids succeed.* But we know that great players aren't always great coaches. They forget their early training in a *traditional* public school and perhaps credit only their own genius for their success.

Celebrities also take unwitting (and unfair) advantage of the benefits that charters have—hurdles to admission that weed out and reject students and parents who are not conscientious; no requirement to court the children of local residents or even make the school's presence known to them; the ability to leverage the celebrity of their famous backers to raise money or secure local community and political support. These advantages may ensure that their individual school is a success, but the school undermines the system as a whole by exacerbating the brain drain—and the drain of well-behaved students—from poor areas. Similarly, living as we do in a celebrity-driven culture, the public warms to charters because they find it easy to transfer their admiration for Zuckerberg's or Diddy's or Agassi's success in their respective fields to their efforts in education, without being aware of the pitfalls and the obstacles charters create. We just assume these famous people are acting heroically and not doing anything to harm the system. A traditional public school named after Harriet Tubman seems lackluster and outdated compared to the glamour of a school founded by P. Diddy.

While I was writing this book, a friend of mine, a principal at a charter school, was attempting to renew her school's charter. Curious about the process, I asked her how her sponsors determine whether authorizing the opening of a new school will lead to market saturation. Her answer was that the sponsors don't; she does, by downloading general census numbers from the internet. This was in 2017. The last census was in 2010. This is far from the market precision one needs for a market to thrive. Consequently, the market for charters hit the saturation point eons ago. (By contrast, in normal market enterprises like Starbucks, it can be determined with ruthless precision where to authorize the opening of a new store. In fact, an entire branch of the Seattle-based company, equipped with "20 or so analytics experts around the world poring over maps and geographic information systems data—assessing factors like an area's traffic patterns and businesses," is dedicated to figuring out exactly where the newest of its nineteen thousand franchises will be located. There is nothing approaching this type of precision in the charter-school version of market analysis.)[10]

Yet in many portions of the country, and despite the baleful warnings of teacher shortages, supply is now driving demand. Teach for America has to find a place for the five thousand teachers it trains each year (as do other teacher-training nonprofits and schools), so with its powerful national allies it pushes for more and more charters, more and more competition for already thinly spread dollars, weakening the infrastructure, with tiny struggling school after tiny struggling school competing for bodies (not minds) just to keep the battered doors open and the blinking lights on.

At one sorely underfunded charter where I worked, I volunteered to hire and pay an SAT tutor for a group of seniors who had hardly even heard of the test. I advertised for the job, saying I would pay $50 an hour to someone of quality. My efforts (unintentionally) embarrassed the principal, who brought me into his office, pulled out his tiny school's budget, and told me with some anguish that he had "found the money" to help pay for the tutor. I countered that I was happy to foot the bill. As a kid, I'd found an SAT course that was offered about thirty miles from my home. I got up every Saturday at six in the morning and drove my parents' old station wagon to the class, which began at eight. Had I not done so, I'd never have been able to score even half-decently on the test. I was happy to pay whatever it took to help these students. But the principal was a proud man and insisted on splitting the costs, despairing that he couldn't do more, in large part because another tiny charter had recently opened up down the road and he was already losing students (money) to it. Six charter high schools had set up shop within a two-mile radius of his school. I don't know which important bill went unpaid so this principal could send poor black and Latino seniors (who could never afford to pay for the SAT test, let alone a tutor, on their own) into the test with some idea of what to expect, but no school should have to make such choices.

The CFO of a well-known, but still struggling, charter school in Los Angeles has kept his school many millions of dollars in the black for years. But the school struggles to hire teachers because it pays below market rate. Why? Because the executive was trained in the private sector and believes all private companies should have millions in unspent cash on hand. Never mind that the library stood empty of books, that the SAT class had no one trained in the SAT to teach how to take it, that there was no sports field or French class or shop, or orchestra or teacher stability, and that it took ages to get a kid removed from class because not enough campus personnel were available to deal with unruly kids. The profit-oriented CFO prevented the school from spending on those basic needs or even paying teachers decent salaries. The charter school years have been years of magical thinking.

So what now? How do we take the hard lessons learned from the traditional schools and the best of charter schools and make public education work better? How can we harness the power of the free market to be of true benefit to public schools? First, no more charter schools should be opened. A strict moratorium on them is long overdue. Then let's test all students. Those charter schools whose students are doing markedly better than those in the regular school system (despite the unfairness of their advantage) should remain open (for now). Charter schools whose students are doing as well as or worse than their public school counterparts should be closed and merged into larger schools. This would afford larger schools the economies of scale a school needs to absorb the financial shocks that come with losing students (to illness or suspension or family moves) without placing the very running of the school in jeopardy.

As far as competition, we should let charter organizations compete to offer the reformed reform schools I wrote of earlier. Rather than fighting to teach the best students, let them innovate and experiment with how to reach the toughest, the least socialized, the most angry. The deep pockets of philanthropists can help staff these new charters with the best amenities and staff—teachers, counselors, therapists, and aides—that private money can buy.* Model them after schools like Liahona Preparatory Academy in Utah or the Glen Mills Schools in Pennsylvania, which boast a 65 percent success rate at keeping kids who have had brushes with the law from returning to any form of illegal activity. Offer group therapy and individual therapy; instruct them daily in impulse control and anger management. Teach them to fix cars *and* to conjugate verbs so, as Rousseau counseled, they have something that occupies their bodies and their minds. Staff these schools with a thousand Betty Hugheses, she who taught the opera singer Ryan Speedo Green in a special class for kids with anger problems when he was nine, remembered him years later, and saw to it that he was given a chance to sing. Throw the light of day on these schools so that qualified social scientists and community leaders can keep a keen eye on the school and report what they see. All this would be aimed at giving the toughest kids a second and third and even fourth chance at finding their way. And we can leave the now reconstituted larger schools, which should also be free to tap private wealth to augment their budgets, to be the mixture of gems and knuckleheads that large schools need to be a thriving and stimulating place for kids to learn and grow.

What happened at the start of the new semester with Rodiney dismayed me. A little more than halfway through the previous semester, Rodiney had fallen in with Dayshawn and Greg. They were all on the basketball team, and the discipline and comity Dayshawn and Greg practiced with and extended to each other transferred to Rodiney. The one or two occasions I subbed in a class with

* There are currently strict regulations on donating private money directly to schools, but these regulations are worth reevaluating and updating for the sorely underfunded schools in economically depressed areas whose low property taxes put them at a permanent disadvantage to schools in wealthier areas.

all three of them during the end of the first semester, I saw the change. Rodiney had adopted their good nature and easy confidence. It was, I'm sure, why he and I began getting along better. He was a knucklehead who'd fallen in with gems. He did his work, never cursed (that I could hear), apologized immediately when he irritated me ("My bad, Mr."), and developed an adolescent joy in making other people laugh. He wasn't as funny as Dayshawn, but he wasn't embarrassed to try.

But at the very end of the first semester, Rodiney was cut from the basketball team for being late to practice too many times, and with that, his demeanor soured and it never seemed to recover. By the time the new semester started and I took over teaching full time, a rift had grown between him and Greg. Dayshawn, I learned, tried to mediate, but it didn't work. Eventually, Dayshawn sided with his best friend. I tried to find out a little more of what had happened, thinking maybe I could help smooth things between them, but adults are fundamentally guests in the kingdom of kids. Their language is not fully decipherable, and you rely on their goodwill to grant you safe passage. Pressing them too hard for their secrets is like asking them to give up intel to a foreign power. You'll ultimately be expelled and they'll close their borders to you for good. So I let it be and was crestfallen when, during the second week of the new semester, Rodiney had moved out of Honors History and into my sixth-period class, where he was within the reach of Erik. Dayshawn and Greg had released Rodiney from their protective power. Rodiney would be on his own.

9

What It Means to Be Distracted

Harrison was taken from his parents, George and Hazel, as an adolescent. He had shown a promise they didn't have, an unhappiness with the status quo, and, to the watchful eye, a willingness to act on that unhappiness. Harrison crossed the line. The Ministry of Equality was displeased.

Ethan Adshade woke up babbling. He had started teaching at Cullen less than a month earlier, and now it had happened again. This was becoming routine. The last thing he remembered was falling asleep while rehearsing the next day's lesson in his head. And within five hours he'd awakened from a dream while mouthing gibberish. He had been trying to solve math problems in his sleep. Math problems that didn't exist: What is the sine greater when not non x? If y is equal to y, solve for the equal sign. Zero times zero is the rooted cube of which pigeon? Each time, it took him a while to clear his mind and calm himself. He looked at the time, still two hours before his alarm was set to go off. He had no chance of going back to sleep now. He climbed out of bed and padded over to where his giant mastiff lay sleeping. He didn't want to disturb him. But Ethan had felt a sense of helplessness closing in on him for the past few weeks, and hearing his dog's slow breathing on these restless mornings helped calm him. Ethan could already feel his classes slipping away. Behavior-wise nearly all could be a challenge.

1st period—Early morning truancies kept the classroom fairly manageable.

2nd period–Planning.

3rd period—He'd had to send Miguel and Nacho out of class the day before. They'd almost gotten into a fight.

4th period—It had its bad days. He had kicked Carlos out for rolling a blunt in class.

6th period—If Esmerelda and Guadalupe weren't there, things were good.

But fifth period was sheer madness and Shayla was its undisputed leader. She was pretty, popular, and the girlfriend of Derek, the baddest dude at Cullen not named Percy. She ran the school. Always with the latest Air Jordans, the flyest gear, and bling enough to embarrass Betelgeuse, the second-brightest star in Orion. By the end of the year she would turn out to be a true gem, but he saw no evidence of that now, so early in the year. Her true character was buried deep beneath a welter of anger and resentment, at whom Ethan hadn't the faintest idea. He noticed that Shayla exploded most often when she was frustrated with the work, and, in math at least, she was nearly always frustrated. Other students had no specific trigger point that he could discern. (He hated the frequent claim that students would behave if your lessons were good. That was just another slander aimed at teachers. You could plan the greatest lesson in the world, but if a kid was in a bad mood that day, it didn't matter. Truth was, sometimes it was impossible to know what could set a kid off. Of course the time Dejon told Bernard he looked like the Hamburglar, and the whole class started laughing, the trigger was obvious. Bernard tackled him in the middle of class. But, then, Bernard did look like the Hamburglar and had just told Dejon that he had digitally probed Dejon's mother the night before.)

As Ethan dressed and got ready for school, he remembered what had happened a week earlier after he'd thrown a random question into a worksheet about converting a decimal into a fraction. Next to no one had answered it. He had wanted to go back and review that but he was on a strict schedule. Cullen's charter district maintained a rigid timeline teachers had to follow, moving through math objectives at a steady clip. Finding the slope was on the menu for at least the next week. He had broached the subject at the end of class the day before, and the kids seemed to struggle with the concept. But he'd attack things anew today. As he headed to work, though, the decimal question lurked in the back of his mind. The slope of a line is rise over run. How far a line goes up over how far it goes over. The kids understood the y-intercept, the coefficient, and the integers; the m in $y = mx + b$ was what seemed to stump them. He called the places where things break down, where kids start to get confused and need help, bottlenecks. Decimals were the bottlenecks a few weeks earlier and slope had been the bottleneck yesterday.

Ethan stood at the back of the classroom with the lights out, the projector throwing his PowerPoint in patterns on the screen, while decimals and slope rambled about in his mind. As he walked through the class, asking questions that got a muted response at best, he could feel himself tracing the edge of the problem. He flashed an equation on the screen. The class was quiet for a minute or two as his mind pressed on the bottleneck—*decimals and slope, decimals and slope.* And then he heard Shayla quietly whisper to Stacey next to her, "You wanna get kicked out?"

Ethan whipped around. "No!"

"What?!" They looked up, stunned.

"I heard you! Do not try and get kicked out right now. You're gonna stay here and do this work." Ethan gave them his meanest teacher face as they chuckled and refocused on the work. But during those few seconds, something in Ethan had been punted aside. It wasn't until he asked a kid to express the slope of the line close to the end of class that he had a breakthrough. *Fractions! That was it!* His students were tenth-graders, but they didn't understand the concept of fractions! That was what linked slope and decimals. Converting a decimal means building a fraction. And slope is expressed as a fraction, rise over run. They were lost.

If my brief stint as a sub taught me I had any gift as a teacher, it was one I had recognized immediately in Ethan and the other great teachers with whom I came in contact: the ability to see a question in its most elemental form, to sense the question under the question. His students didn't understand slope because they didn't understand fractions. And they didn't understand fractions because they didn't understand that a small number can be divided by a bigger number, the whole of which a fraction is a part.

The strongest reason I had for taking the long-term assignment of preparing a few Cullen seniors for the California High School Exit Examination (CAHSEE) was that students had told me several times, "You explain it better than our teacher." It didn't happen often—I subbed for some great teachers—but it gave me confidence when it did. The ability to suss out where confusion lies—the obstruction, the bottleneck—like finding where something is stuck in a pipe, then identifying the obstruction—is the central ability of good teachers. Their main skill is then to slowly build a bridge, piece by piece, toward the child's understanding. Any and everything else is icing on the cake.

Consider the opening paragraph of *The Scarlet Letter*:

It is a little remarkable, that—though disinclined to talk overmuch of myself and my affairs at the fireside, and to my personal friends—an autobiographical impulse should twice in my life have taken possession of me, in addressing the public. The first

time was three or four years since, when I favoured the reader—
inexcusably, and for no earthly reason that either the indulgent
reader or the intrusive author could imagine—with a description
of my way of life in the deep quietude of an Old Manse. And
now—because, beyond my deserts, I was happy enough to find a
listener or two on the former occasion—I again seize the public
by the button, and talk of my three years' experience in a Custom-
House.

Greeted by this level of archaic language, most high school students
(and perhaps most adults too) feel daunted. I had to teach this passage one day in an Honors English class and, fortunately, I knew
what to do. Once class started, I told the students to take out their
pencils and put brackets around everything inside the dashes, then
read the passage again but skip everything in brackets. This is how
it read anew:

It is a little remarkable, that an autobiographical impulse should
twice in my life have taken possession of me, in addressing the
public. The first time was three or four years since, when I favoured the reader with a description of my way of life in the
deep quietude of an Old Manse. And now I again seize the public by the button, and talk of my three years' experience in a
Custom-House.

I forgot who taught me that trick, but the difference is almost magical. I was helping them boil down the book to its essence before
asking them to appreciate its art. I knew the bottleneck—the
obstacle—was the ornate language and the abundance of words,
so stripping it to its core was the bridge to their understanding.
This was the only way to help any student struggling with reading
see the book, and that passage in particular, for what it was. But
the process of doing this is a delicate one and goes by a fancy name:

phenomenology. To understand the nature of the learning process, it's important you know what phenomenology is.

The most famous line of phenomenology you've actually heard before: "I think, therefore I am." What it means is that the content of my mind is the most important thing about my identity as a human being; my understanding of *how* and *what* to think as well as how I perceive myself and the world around me—my very consciousness—is the single most valuable aspect of my existence. I think, therefore I am. But thinking in thoughts, as one of the greatest phenomenologists insists, is for most of us thinking in language, and that matters.

In some ways you already know this. Picture it: you're in your kitchen, idly preparing a meal, when your daughter enters to check the fridge. As you're pouring the rice into the pot, you suddenly hear her say, "What did you say?" You look over at her confused and take a second to realize what happened. You smile sheepishly and say, "Oh, I was just talking to myself." Your daughter caught you while you were mumbling your thoughts out loud; the mumbling she heard was the outer version of the inner speech going on in your head. Scholars of human consciousness (phenomenologists) tell us that the character of this inner speech—which is happening every moment of every day, even when we are sleeping—is what defines us as humans.

As Ethan was teaching slope, standing at the back of the class and quietly trying to solve the puzzle of his students' confusion, he was engaging in inner speech. While he was flashing slides on the board, his mind was saying the words *slope* and *decimals* over and over and quietly asking what they had in common, until he had a eureka moment and realized it was fractions. And from there his mind spun off into a different inner dialogue to figure out how to best teach fractions—to build a bridge toward his students. It's this stream of consciousness, always rushing, always coursing, always branching off into a thousand different tributaries, that makes each individual both unique and just like every other member of the human family.

Using outward speech to prod and direct a child's inner speech is what adults do when they teach. After telling a child to carry the four a hundred times, we want it to become a permanent part of her inner speech, so that when she confronts a math problem anew, her inner voice will prompt her to say silently to herself, "Carry the four." When students go from reading out loud to reading silently, or when they go from counting on their fingers to counting in their head, they have achieved a developmental advance, a deepening of their consciousness. (To see middle school students still counting on their fingers or mouthing words as they read is painful; you know the development of their inner speech—their consciousness— has been stunted somewhere along the way.) But no matter what we are doing, inner speech accompanies it, to match and narrate and guide our effort. Inner speech is the voice of identity creation. The construction of a child's inner speech—whether about math or racism or the latest hit movie—is the construction of a child's humanity.

But identity construction—the line from an adult's outer speech to the child's inner speech—is a terribly fragile thing. A poem by Walt Whitman encapsulates what it means to cast the thin and fragile line from the mind of a teacher into the mind of a child. In such a transaction the mind and soul of a teacher moves with the care and fragility of a "noiseless, patient spider":

I mark'd where on a little promontory it stood isolated
Mark'd how to explore the vacant vast surrounding
It launch'd forth filament, filament, filament, out of itself, Ever
    unreeling them, ever tirelessly speeding them
. . .
Ceaselessly musing, venturing, throwing, seeking the spheres to
    connect them.

Till the bridge you will need be form'd, till the ductile anchor
  hold,
Till the gossamer thread you fling catch somewhere, O my soul.[1]

The proper creation of a child's consciousness—of his intellectual and moral capacity—demands, at moments, quiet (*noiseless, isolated, vacant and vast*) and time (*ever unreeling, ceaselessly*), so that the gossamer thread that an adult sends from quiet mind to quiet mind has a chance to catch somewhere. And this is true of all concentrated acts of learning or thinking, whether a teacher is present or not.

When Barack Obama was in office, he said what he missed most about civilian life was having the time to think things through. When he was preparing to leave office, he said he wanted to go away and "be quiet for a while." Time and quiet.

When a student approached the great naturalist Louis Agassiz with hopes of studying under him, Agassiz tested the student's powers of observation by promptly placing a fish in front of him and left him in a lab [quiet] for three days [time] to list every part of the fish he could see with his naked eye.

Toni Morrison tells of a student who only in grad school learned he suffered from a terrible disability: he'd "never learned to sit in a room by himself and read for four hours and have those four hours followed by another four [time] without any companionship but his own mind [quiet]."[2]

Helen Vendler wrote of studying under the great I. A. Richards, the British educator and literary critic: "Richards entered the Hall in Harvard Yard where the large poetry course was to be held, saw the overcrowded room with undergraduates seated on the floor, heard the fire siren shrieking from the Broadway fire station . . . and moved the class to the quiet of Radcliffe." The students sat in silence for the entire duration [time] of the class as Richards lectured with his back to them, analyzing every word of a poem he'd pro-jected onto a screen.[3]

The writer J. D. Vance, who rocketed to fame for his memoir of "hillbilly folk," described the experience that saved his life: leaving the violence and chaos of his mother's home as a teen and moving in with his fierce but loving grandmother. His grades started to improve and his emotional IQ grew too: "Those three years [time] with Mamaw—uninterrupted and alone [quiet]—saved me."[4]

Although those two poles of knowledge (and self-) creation aren't necessary at all moments of the learning process, when they are, they are absolutely necessary. They are the baseline.

As Ethan stood at the back of the classroom, desperately scanning his students' body language, listening to the hesitation in their voices, sensing like a blind but sensitive mole the source of the obstruction that was hindering them, he needed that baseline, the time and quiet. At that moment any tremor other than the tremor of intellectual hesitation, any noise other than the noise of intellectual confusion, would have prevented him from hearing the idea quietly emerging in his mind—*Fractions! They don't understand fractions!* That was why he barked so suddenly at Shayla, who was preparing to cause a scene. When a teacher is struggling to launch a filament into the minds of his students, he needs to have "a hush come over the crowd," as an art teacher at an Episcopal school where I subbed quietly told his seventh-graders. (The art teacher was quoting the apostle Paul's speech about his journey to Damascus.) This is a first principle. Without the most basic ability to hush the crowd when it needs to be hushed, no learning gets done, the anchor never holds.

This came home to me with Junior—you know, Pusillanimous Junior. A few years after I left Cullen, I visited my former colleagues and students. Many teachers I'd known had left, and the school had cycled through several principals while I'd been gone. I was nevertheless happy to see students who were now a bit older, more mature. At one point I asked about Junior, whom I had not yet seen. Life had not gone well for him. The previous year he'd been goofing off in a math class. Another student, Jabari, a bright and conscientious kid, whom I'd also known, was at the board struggling to figure out an algebra problem. The teacher, someone I didn't know, was standing at the board with Jabari, guiding, nudging, launching one filament after another as he tried to point Jabari toward the right answer. But the teacher was a first-year and still struggled with classroom management at a school that offered little help with classroom management. And many first-years were reluctant to send students out of class lest it reflect poorly on the teacher.

Apparently, the math teacher, Ralph Contreras, had warned Junior several times to settle down, but he wouldn't quit. Jabari, for his part, couldn't focus and, feeling helpless and frustrated, finally yelled, "Junior, please! I have you in every class! I can never figure anything out!" The class went silent and an embarrassed Junior tried to rush Jabari, but Contreras stood between them, so Junior pushed Contreras, trying to knock him into Jabari. Contreras fell over. Contreras pressed the issue and Junior was ultimately expelled.

This story crushed me, for many reasons: the damage to Junior, a kid I liked and rooted for, a classic knucklehead but without enough self-discipline (or school-based discipline) to tame his wilder instincts. And it didn't take much. He was harmless but because of the absence of intermediate punishments, he pushed the boundaries until he received the worst punishment. And there was, of course, the damage to Jabari and kids like him whom I knew to be respectful and ambitious but who could not concentrate because the Juniors of the world were constantly disrupting their chain of thought—taking away the time and quiet they needed to push through a difficult problem. Strangely, I had previously only thought of how disruptions shattered *my* train of thought, having to reestablish order, start over, refocus on whatever problem I was trying to help the students solve. I had not thought, until then, about how the *students'* train of thought is shattered too.

(This is yet another negative aspect of small schools. Kids are constantly together with the same cohort of students in every class, year after year. If the group dynamics are good and work well, then kids thrive. If the group dynamics aren't, then kids suffer.)

The American phenomenologist Don Ihde, who wrote most persuasively about inner speech, asked this basic question: Is it possible to turn off inner speech? And Junior, his more chaotic instincts unchecked, regularly short-circuited Jabari's and Contreras's inner speech. Ihde says, "A momentary turn-off may occur in certain types of shock experiences. A loud sonic boom or blind flashing light may temporarily so shock me that my 'thought is lost.'"[5] Science has recently confirmed what we all have intuited to be true: interruptions cause us to make mistakes. A study, "Momentary Interruptions Can Derail the Train of Thought," found that interruptions averaging 4.4 seconds tripled the rate of errors in adults who were performing a basic sequential task and that interruptions lasting 2.8 seconds doubled the rate of errors.[6] All math is a sequential task and so are English and reading.

The study's subjects were competent, educated adults. High school students' minds are still developing, so disruptions of their chain of thought often last longer than the disruptions found in the study. I've become more and more convinced that those notorious "gaps in learning" are as much a result of endless disruptions in chaotic environments as they are the result of unqualified teachers incapable of helping students in the first place. While I was teaching I sometimes was amazed at the bizarre things a student didn't know. Such as the twelfth-grader taking honors classes who didn't know what a glossary or an index is. (Does anyone really think a college-educated teacher didn't know or try to teach that?) In the course of a single hour's class, the disruptions from students with no impulse control, who can't be suspended or given detention or sent to the principal's office, make that class one long disruption.

Try it yourself. Set an alarm to ring loudly or to flash brightly every ten seconds or so as you try to solve the following five problems. This is middle school work:

1. $(9 - 1 \cdot 2) \cdot 8 =$
2. $5 \cdot 6 - 3 \cdot (-6) =$
3. Solve $12 + 16q - q^4$ when $q = 2$
4. $(x + 4) - 20/4$, when $x = 4$
5. $[(x - 2)^2 + 3]/3$, when $x = 5$

Maybe you've forgotten the order of operations, or maybe you vaguely remember and want to try it on your own. Maybe you're a gem and the student next to you is a gem too, but maybe the kid in front of you is a knucklehead and his best friend is being an asshole, and right now they're both arm-wrestling and talking shit. Maybe you need the teacher's help, but you're kind of shy and a teacher's aide told your mom when you were younger that you have a form of dyslexia, even though no one ever officially tested you, and either way you don't want to draw attention to yourself by raising your hand in this class, especially because none of the girls in the next row likes you or your friend, and they always mock you when they see you raising your hand. Two other kids are looking at a video on a phone of the fight on the bus this morning, and now they're passing it around the class, and everyone who sees it starts bugging out and laughing. And if you're honest, even though you're supposed to be trying to figure out the order of operations, you want to see the video too. The teacher hears the ruckus and yells at one of the kids to put the phone away or she's going to confiscate it, and the kid says, "You not taking shit." The teacher yells at him to watch his language and tries to call the guard but the wall phone doesn't work, so the kids keep passing the phone around because teachers really don't have any power to take anyone's phone anyway and everyone knows it.

You try to go back to figuring out the problem on your own and check your answer against your friend's, but her answer is different from yours. You try to read the textbook but, truth is, the book is really hard to understand and it's easier for you when the teacher explains things. But the teacher is still helping another kid, and about six other kids had their hand up before you did, and the kid the teacher is helping takes forever to learn things, because he actually got an F in math last year and probably shouldn't even be in eighth-grade math. And then another kid who doesn't belong in the classroom runs in, turns out the light, yells, "Fuck y'all," and runs off. Everyone starts laughing and going, "Oooooooohhh!" and the teacher, who is at the other end of the room, has to yell over the laughter to ask someone to please turn the light back on. Of course, no one does so the teacher walks over in the dark to turn it on, and now the look on her face says she's had enough.

And for a second you're the teacher, and you're standing there looking at your class, knowing at least a dozen or more kids still need your help, but you can't get this class to be quiet to save your life. You'd call their parents, but you're exhausted at the end of the day and just want to get the hell out of school and not think about this place until tomorrow, and it hardly ever works when you call some parents anyway. And since you're a new teacher with your first-year evaluation coming up, and the principal blames you when your classes are misbehaving, even though you've tried every strategy she's suggested and none of it seems to work, you're doubting whether you have any business trying to be a teacher at all, even though you loved your teachers as a kid and always dreamed of being one. You just don't know if you're cut out for this.

But some kids still have their hands up, and you're not even through helping the kid who failed math last year. Do you go back over to try to help someone who is so far behind that it just feels like a waste of time? Also, last week he cursed at you and you're still a little skittish around him. And what about the kid who never raises her hand because she's kind of shy? Does she need help? You've sent an email to the school's sole counselor expressing your concern that the student might have a learning disability, but that was more than three weeks ago and you still have not received a response. A glance at the board and you suddenly realize that you wrote one of the problems incorrectly. How the hell did you make that mistake? You know the fucking order of operations, but sometimes it can be hard for even you to focus. Should you try to explain it again, even though no one is listening? Somewhere in your brain you remember learning that the word *distraction* comes from an old Latin word that means "shattered into pieces," and that's honestly how you feel some days. And now the campus aides are coming up the stairs quickly, which is good because maybe they can take the kid's phone, but you realize that they're heading to another classroom, where a fight has broken out. So never mind that. The truth is that you're standing in the doorway and just waiting for the bell to ring at this point, so you can take the fifteen-minute break you get between second and third periods. You'll get to at least put your head down for a little while, even though it is still early in the day. Your next class is your seventh-graders and they're really hell on wheels.

Students who are raised in chaotic environments can become conditioned to crave the sound of chaos. The silence of a quiet classroom induces in these students a type of panic. But if we have any chance of vanquishing that terror, of saving both the Juniors and the Jabaris, we need to think in both philosophical and practical ways about the inordinately high costs of chaos and disruptions to the development of the cognitive mind.

This train of thought has a counterpart in fiction, a powerful one, the Kurt Vonnegut short story "Harrison Bergeron," which I referenced at the opening of this chapter. In the dystopian fantasy the United States has become an authoritarian state, and ominous bureaucracies like the Ministry of Equality and the United States Handicapper General govern every aspect of human life. People who show any promise or talent or intelligence or, especially, an appetite for resistance are monitored, hobbled, and even imprisoned by the state. They are outfitted with, among other things, "a little mental handicap radio in their ears" that is tuned to a government transmitter, and every twenty seconds it "send[s] out some sharp noise to keep them from taking unfair advantage of their brains."[7]

When the state takes Harrison, then fourteen, from his parents, his father, George, who once had evinced intelligence like his son's, "couldn't think about it very hard" because when he tried "a buzzer sounded" in his head and sent thoughts "[fleeing] in panic, like bandits from a burglar alarm." Whenever George's inner voice had an opportunity to develop a thought of sadness or feeling of anger or memory of the past, a loud noise chased it from his mind. When he thought about Harrison in jail, "a twenty-one-gun salute in his head stopped that." When George stopped to ponder the nature of beauty, "another noise in his ear radio scattered his thoughts." When his wife is stumped by a question, George can't answer because "a siren was going off in his head." Each time George's inner voice had to start over from the beginning. The state has weaponized distraction, taking away people's time and quiet, forcing them to think the same thought over and over from the beginning.

A mirror image of this nightmare exists in the real world. It is best seen in the memoirs of black men who tell, terrifyingly, of being able to find the peace and quiet they need to develop their mind and spirit only behind the bars of a prison cell. Malcolm X found only in prison the peace and quiet that led him to the duties of religious and intellectual devotion. John Lewis, who was hit on the head by police batons more times than he could count, took a book with him to each protest; he'd get the chance to read it once he'd been put in jail. Martin Luther King Jr. literally wrote "Letter from a Birmingham Jail" from that jail: "What else can one do when he is alone in a narrow jail cell but . . . think long thoughts?" The cousin of a famous black scholar was only able to get the time and quiet to finish his GED in prison. Within a year of being released from prison, he was killed. A man convicted of murder and sentenced to life in prison began to read Frederick Douglass and wrote long, beautiful letters to his daughter.

This is a cause for panic. When the seventeenth-century poet George Herbert wrote, "Happier the hands fettered than the mind distracted," it was with the defiant irony of a parish priest who had freely chosen his confinement. Herbert could have walked free anytime he chose, but his remark can be read as the most baleful comment possible about how fully the bodies and souls of "free" black youth are menaced (by street and police violence, by fetish of prurient whites, by poverty and self-immolation, and by chaotic schools) such that their only escape from distraction—from being literally and spiritually pulled apart—is too often under the dangerous gaze of a prison guard. This cannot be the fate to which we leave the poor, black or otherwise. Despite Herbert, a free mind, for a free people, cannot possibly be born of fettered hands and feet.

At the end of "Harrison Bergeron," the young Harrison has broken out of prison. He has somehow managed to strip the massive earphones from his head along with the glasses with thick, wavy lenses designed to blind him, to discard the heavy bags of scrap metal that weighed him down, and the massive harness that encased his head. He has found his way onto a state-run television broadcast as the world watches him. Inspired by his defiance, the people around him rip off their headsets and tear off their harnesses. As his parents watch this unfold on TV, they become vaguely aware that they are watching their son. When the state police finally catch up with Harrison, they shoot and kill him. The revolution, televised, dies before it's born. His mother drops a tear at the sight of her murdered son, but George, his memory of his son blasted from his mind, has wandered off.

When George returns from the kitchen with a beer he asks his wife if she's been crying.

> "Yup," she said.
>
> "What about?" he said.
>
> "I forget," she said. "Something real sad on television."
>
> "What was it?" he said.
>
> "It's all kind of mixed up in my mind," said Hazel.
>
> "Forget sad things," said George.
>
> "I always do," said Hazel.
>
> "That's my girl," said George. He winced. There was the sound of a riveting gun in his head.[8]

"Mixed up in my mind," indeed. Children learning and developing in a world of endless distraction are having their souls and consciousness literally torn apart. If we cannot find a way to subdue the chaos, *truth*, *knowledge*, *equality*, *fractions*, *affection*, and *freedom* will forever just be meaningless words, mixed up in their minds.

10

Forget It, Jake. It's Chinatown.

In these pages I have tried to explain what I believe to be the various strands of social, economic, psychological, and even legal forces that have crippled America's poorest schools and its most vulnerable students: the crack cocaine epidemic and the expanding "rights of the child"; the eradication of the most commonsense forms of stringency (detention, suspension, quality "reform" schools, or simple gestures like sending kids to the principal's office); the explosion of white liberal fascination with race, sex, and thuggery and its impact on the minds of black boys in all-white environments; the absence of father figures who can physically subdue a hormonal adolescent boy's belief in his own maturity; the crude attempt to graft free-market ideas onto a public good; the obsession with forcing "disruptive" new ideas onto communities that have already been woefully disrupted by drugs, poverty, and violence; the high cost of endless distractions to the development of human consciousness.

I have spent long hours in conversation and thought as well as chance meetings, dead ends, and redirections to build a plausible case for the contribution of each of these factors. But as I wind up the story of my year in public schools, I want to provide a brief look at how a teacher feels when the official party line from every quarter—politicians, parents, school administrators, education experts, the media—never mentions any of these issues and focuses only on a teacher's failure. To be a teacher today is to feel yourself locked in a carnival funhouse with trapdoors, two-way mirrors, and instructions for escape written in disappearing ink.

You may not have noticed the most famous example of this, but every teacher in the country did. Ask yourself what it means to be "in receive mode." I'll give you a minute. Maybe you think it's simple—everyone knows what it means to receive something, right? But what does it mean to be in the mode to receive? Maybe you think about how a walkie-talkie is in receive mode when you release the talk button right after you've finished speaking. But imagine that someone has told you that *you* are in receive mode and, more, that person is insulting you when she says it. What mistake could you have made such that you, a person, had inappropriately been in a mode to receive? Maybe you're in a leadership training program and your instructor wanted you to take charge, but you were too passive? You didn't assert yourself enough?

This is the baffling question I asked myself when a local public school in Washington, DC, Jefferson Academy, opened its doors to the secretary of education, who'd just been appointed to the most powerful government post in education. Betsy DeVos had spent the morning there, welcomed by teachers and students. After she left, a national reporter interviewed her about the visit. The education secretary said that the teachers she'd met were all wildly talented and committed, to be sure, but unfortunately all seemed to be "in receive mode" and that wasn't going to help students succeed.[1] I had no idea what those words meant, except that I knew she was insulting them. And so did the teachers. The academy's administrators lashed out on Twitter, providing a long list of all the innovative things the teachers had initiated and concluded, "[Our] teachers are not in a 'receive' mode. Unless you mean we 'receive' students at a 2nd grade level and move them to an 8th grade level."[2] Use of the phrase "unless you mean" shows the administrators were as dumbfounded by the critique as I was.

When I dug deeper to see if there was a way to parse the secretary's words, they seemed only slightly less confusing and every bit as insulting. She seemed to be saying that these were the type of teachers who were waiting to be told what to do rather than taking the initiative to do whatever their students needed. For the record, a nonsense phrase, to me, is not just one that is weird or unintelligible but one that you are helpless to address or truly refute because it is unintelligible.

"In receive mode" carries a permanent taint but points to no recognizable way to remedy the perception. After all, what could the teachers possibly have done that would have told the secretary that they were *not* in receive mode while in the very act of welcoming (receiving) her? Should they not have received her at all? Or been rude during the reception? Failed or refused to acknowledge the secretary's presence when she walked into their rooms? Openly disagreed with any point she made? How could they have asserted themselves at the time? How should they assert themselves if she ever decides to come back? Should they wear hats that say, "Not in receive mode"?

There's a reason that I am dwelling on the nonsense, the weird, illogical, anodyne, but sometimes openly mendacious nonsense. It bothers me because I think that it is the invisible ingredient that tips teachers into the modern version of hysteria. It goes by less archaic names today—exhaustion, burnout—but the lifelessness of it, the soullessness of it, represents a type of spiritual and mental collapse inside the mind of a teacher who suddenly wakes up one morning and says, "I can't do this anymore."

Every few months a new headline speaks to the shortage of public school teachers as more and more people flee the profession at younger and younger ages. While people may give up other careers—acting, singing, boxing—and then return, when people give up teaching today, they almost never come back. Why is that? Because of the anger and frustration that the nonsense words create in you. A Russian poet, I forget who, wrote that language—clear, accurate, and honest language—is a society's best weapon against insanity. And the language of education will drive you crazy.

A recent article in *Slate* magazine that drew my skeptical attention was "To Improve School Discipline, Change *Teacher* Behavior." The article focused on a new teacher, David, who had been having a tough time teaching math to ninth-graders. The school district had assigned him an "instructional reform facilitator" to help him alter his classroom behavior. David seemed to be having an especially difficult time with a kid named John, who apparently caused the most trouble. The reporter describes the day the facilitator visits and observes David's teaching: the kids have their cell phones out, other kids are listening to music on their headphones, still others are sword fighting with rulers, and John suddenly walks out of class without permission and sings loudly while David is trying to teach. When David met with the facilitator after class for advice about how to get his class on track, she tells him "the pacing was off" in his lesson.[3] You'd have to work in teaching to know this is a common complaint from evaluators, one that is utterly ridiculous.

Keep in mind that there are no tracks in America's public schools anymore—a ninth-grade math class could include a kid with a fourth-grade understanding of math sitting next to a kid with eleventh-grade comprehension and could be dotted with every level in between. Given that, how can David fix his pace? Should he go slower or faster? If a student raises her hand because she is confused and the teacher stops to explain, doesn't that throw off the pace for someone else, who is now bored because she is ready to move on to something more challenging? Is the teacher supposed to ignore the confused student in order to keep "on pace"? Or, what if six kids are confused by the first part of the lesson but ten are confused by the second part, while the rest of the class understands both parts? Is there a pace that fits all of them? The expert offered not a single example or specific to solve David's pace problem. Why? Because this was a problem without a remedy. David didn't create a class with dozens of different academic levels; he was handed it. Yet somehow, the pace was his problem.

Then the expert, according to the reporter, offered David the tautology that if he kept the students engaged most discipline problems would disappear. Of course, if students are engaged, most discipline problems would disappear. Isn't the expert's job to tell David *how* to engage a classroom of kids with different levels of cognitive and behavioral development, interest in the subject, impulse control, and respect for adults? Yet the most she had to say was that the "the pace was off" and that the teacher needed to engage the students better. If the expert asked whether phones could be confiscated or what the school's detention policies were or what happens when David calls home, the reporter made no mention of it. But I've since learned enough about experts to readily doubt any such mention was made. It's much easier for the expert to focus on the unintelligible and unfixable idea of the teacher's bad pacing.

But it got worse. The expert suggested that David "might, unknowingly, be telegraphing a dislike for John, which triggered the student's unhappiness and frustration." This, to my way of thinking, is so slippery and so cutting and yet so perfectly silly at the same time that it borders on genius. How is this teacher supposed to respond to this charge, which is neither provable nor disprovable? What if the teacher's reaction went like this?

David: Dislike? But I like him fine. He's a really smart kid. I just need him to stop cutting up when I'm trying to teach.

Expert: But maybe secretly, subconsciously, you dislike him and he can detect that. Like you said, he's very smart.

David: What? I said smart, not telepathic. John frustrates the hell out of me, but I don't dislike him.

Expert: Again, I'm talking subconsciously.

David: Where are you getting this from? Don't you recognize the difference between being frustrated with someone and disliking him? I get frustrated with my own kids and I yell at them. But it doesn't mean I dislike them.

Expert: Well, kids shouldn't be able to frustrate you. They're kids. You're the adult. If kids have the power to frustrate you, then maybe you're in the wrong profession. And if you're bringing your own parenting strategies into the classroom, maybe you need to examine how you're raising your kids. Either way, I'm sensing a deep-seated hostility in you. Perhaps this is what John is sensing too.

David: I don't have any deep-seated hostility. I just want to know: How can you purport to know what's in my subconscious?

Expert: I said "maybe" and "suggestive of," but it's obvious this has upset you. Is it possible I hit a nerve?

It's. All. Just. Nonsense.

I experienced my own version of this at Cullen and so did Ethan Adshade. He had to prepare his kids to pass the California High School Exit Examination so they could graduate from high school. But the administration eventually called Ethan to the office to tell him: "You're sending too many students out [of class]."

"But I can't teach when they're in my class and won't do as I ask," he replied.

"They're complaining about you; they say you disrespect them."

"How do I disrespect them? I'm trying to teach them," Ethan said.

"It doesn't matter," the principal replied. "Perception is reality, Ethan. If they perceive that you've disrespected them, then that's their reality."

"But what about my perception?" he remonstrated. "I'm the teacher."

"But they're the client. It's their perception that matters."

All these words make a kind of sense, but they are also a negation of reality.

For me the primary problem was Erik. Because he had so much power in his school, I sent him out of class whenever I sensed he was aiming in my direction even a tremor of disrespect. But unchecked assholes stir others up, and I dismissed them from class whenever they, too, stepped out of line or cursed at me. Finally, the new assistant principal called me to his office and told me that I was sending too many kids to the office.

"I can't fight with kids all day," I told him.

"I get that you're a hard-ass," he responded. "I get that you don't like the cursing."

"If a kid curses at me, they're out of my class."

"But there's a difference between a kid saying, 'Fuck that' and 'Fuck you.'"

"If a kid aims the word *fuck* at me in any form, they're out of my class."

"I think the problem, Mr. Henderson, is that you're starting to take this personally."

Is there an answer to that statement that doesn't somehow confirm his suspicion? This is why teachers flee.

But the piece de resistance of the nonsense talk during my year came during a faculty meeting I attended at a middle school. The school had the highest number of students living in group homes. The teacher turnover rate was high. This was a traditional school where the principal had banned teachers from sending students out of class. I knew veteran substitutes who would refuse assignments at Aviation because the kids were so difficult and the administration uncooperative. A teacher I met after working there retired to become an EMT because it was less stressful. Two teachers and an assistant principal would be assaulted by the time I stopped working there. The veterans had complained about the total inability to rein in students so the district sent an expert to help.

We all were crowded into the library after a day of one hallway fight after another. Most teachers had closed and locked their doors to keep kids from running into the middle of their class and turning over chairs or turning off the lights and running out. I was told that someone had set a fire in the upstairs bathroom the week before and by the end of the year three teachers had taken a leave of absence because of the stress of dealing with the unchecked chaos. The principal had requested the district send someone because, she said as she introduced the district expert, "apparently many of you are having a hard time relating to your children." The teachers just stared at her, used to the casual mockery.

The teacher trainer was in her thirties, blond, and could have just as easily been a Wall Street consultant or one of those women you see in lifestyle magazines who have found a way to make wearable clothes out of discarded furniture. All I could think was that this was the wrong person to "train" this group of public school veterans. But I didn't want to pre-judge. I wanted to hear what she had to say. *Maybe it will help*, I thought. She distributed a handout, a story called "The Special Story of Ms. Thompson." It was a doozy. There are several different versions of this story on the internet. But the one that I received was about Ms. Thompson, a fifth-grade teacher who at the start of the school year insisted to her students that she never played favorites and that she saw each student as different from the rest. But there was one student, Teddy, "[she] knew very little about, other than she didn't like him."

The story goes on to describe him as a quiet kid who kept to himself and was poor and disheveled. One day Ms. Thompson searches his school records to see that his former teachers had all described him in glowing terms. The wonderful descriptions continue until the third grade, when the teacher mentions that Teddy is distant because his mother died the previous year and his father was indifferent to him. Then at Christmas that year, the doting students present Ms. Thompson with gifts, Teddy included. But poor boy that he is, Teddy's present was "a gaudy rhinestone bracelet with some stones missing and cheap bottle of perfume." As the kids laugh at Teddy's humble offering, Ms. Thompson quiets them, and sends them home and off to Christmas break at the ringing of the bell. But dear Teddy stays behind and tells Ms. Thompson, "I'm really glad you like my present. My mom's bracelet looks real nice on you and her perfume smells really pretty, too." The story continues, "This comment hit Ms. Thompson so hard, she cried . . . for how badly she had treated him."

This lunatic fairytale—half *The Little Drummer Boy*, half *The Gift of the Magi*—could have been the plot of a 1950s Christmas special: ". . . and now we return to the Hallmark Christmas classic, *The Special Story of Ms. Thompson*," and apparently it was not much different. I Googled the story to find that it had originally run in 1974 in *Home Life* magazine, a religious publication. It was labeled fiction even then. This was what the so-called expert at the second-largest school district in the country had come to this school to train these teachers on. As she read, I looked around the room at the full-time teachers, nearly all of them black or Latino, nearly all of them older than her, some veterans of thirty years, and many of them quite excellent teachers whom I'd come to respect.

Many lived in the neighborhood and had gone to this very school as kids. But most of them had had a day like I'd had, one in which a kid had thrown a chair at another kid, then threw a ruler at me; three fire alarms were pulled; and a seventh-grade student called me a "dick" when I asked him to put his phone away. It was apparently the same student who earlier in the day had called a teacher old enough to be his grandmother "a bitch." But the purveyors of educational nonsense will recount, instead, a nearly fifty-year-old story of an impoverished orphan who was judged harshly and without reason by some awful teacher but despite the teacher's hard heart happened to love her enough to give her the bracelet from his dying mother's hand. Why would anyone need to send Teddy out of class? Or suspend him? He brought his teacher his dead mom's bracelet, for God's sake! There's no way forward as long as the masters of nonsense in American education remain in place.

In some way this chapter represents the end of my intellectual, if not actual, journey through the schools I visited during my year as a substitute—the last surprising peek behind public schools' curtain that I can offer. So I'd like to end the intellectual reach of this book with a final anecdote in the spirit in which I began: a modest notion from the start that convinced me that my hunch was right, that if I trusted what the teachers—the dogged veterans and the hope-filled rookies—were saying, and kept my ear close to the ground, I might be able to figure out what is beneath the surface of troubled schools. Observing this world from ground level would be the best way to see both the forest and the trees.

Proof of that came during the one day I took off while I was working full time at Cullen to do a job I had booked in advance at Aviation. Now I was in a faculty meeting led by Patrick Gordon, the new assistant principal, who was all of thirty years old. He'd just come back from a district training session and was there to teach the teachers how to solve some of the more persistent problems the school was facing. Not a few of the teachers were thirty years his senior, most of them black, and because they were used to being talked down to, they showed no open resistance.

Gordon had brought with him the "Five Whys Protocol," apparently the code cracker of all code crackers. A Google search says it was first used by the Toyota Motor Company "during the evolution of its manufacturing methodologies." I could tell from the temperature in the room that no one was expecting much. The teachers at each table were to identify a persistent problem at the school, ask why it exists, and then keep asking why four more times, until the final root cause was revealed. Gordon went first.

> **Problem: School-wide math scores dropped last year . . . Why is that?**
>
> 1. Teachers did not implement rigorous assessments . . . Why is that?
> 2. Teachers did not understand how to increase classroom rigor . . . Why is that?
> 3. Teachers relied on outdated standards to create assessments . . . Why is that?
> 4. Teachers did not receive any professional instruction about the new standards . . . Why is that?
> 5. The professional development team assumed that lessons were already quite rigorous.

It could have been worse, I suppose. The protocol could have called teachers unqualified or lazy, and almost did, but it could hardly have represented a real effort to root out the problems this tough middle school was facing. But I was sitting at Fred Bailey's table and he was in a mood to do just that. Bailey was as old school a black man as I encountered during my year of subbing. He was partial to the open collars and wingtips of a black man who came of age in the 1970s; at seventy-five he walked with a cane. He had gone to law school at Howard University, alma mater to Toni Morrison, Thurgood Marshall, and Debbie Allen. But jobs for black lawyers were scarce back then, so he got a job teaching history— as an undergrad he had minored in education ("just in case"). When I met him, he was the dean of students at Aviation Middle School, where he had worked for about forty years. And he *was* old school. When I had subbed at Aviation earlier in the year, I had walked into his office one day to hear him quoting Second Corinthians to a kid who was running with the wrong crowd: "Come out ye from among them . . . and be ye separate . . . and I will receive you." Now, during the assistant principal's seminar, Bailey read the trenchant Five Whys that he and his table had come up with:

Problem: Maladaptive behaviors have increased on campus . . . Why is that?

1. So-called experts have created excuses for children/parents, which they readily use . . . Why is that?
2. So-called experts have been/are being paid to invent and/or compile data and invent theories about how to best educate children . . . Why is that?
3. Districts are desperate to please, justify, [and] be held in good standing or high esteem by the privatizers, financial stakeholders, power shakers [sic], and movers . . . Why is that?
4. The financial stakeholders shape public opinion . . . Why is that?
5. People in management positions can be bought and make decisions based on personal benefit and potential profit.

Faculty members quietly muttered, "Preach!" and "Speak now!" and the whole room erupted in applause when he finished. I didn't agree with all of this. Something *did* change in poor communities during the previous thirty years—the children's behaviors weren't maladaptive; they were a natural adaptation to the unnatural things that had happened to them and "experts" and theorists need to think hard about and invent honest theories about how to address them. But everything else—the privatizers, the people in management who can be bought, the so-called experts who prefer nonsense words and verbal traps—was as spot-on as anything I'd ever encountered.

It confirmed for me that others had sensed the complexity I perceived was behind the crisis in public schools. All of which Bailey diagnosed in the span of five lines and a few minutes. It would take me several years and more than two hundred pages to do so. One of the great failures of this country is that Bailey's long-ago law degree from Howard and tendency to quote scripture make him too unglamorous for the cable news circuit or the fancy educational think tanks, which are populated with white PhD students who wouldn't know their way around a tough classroom to save their lives.

Once Bailey was done, it was the turn of Greg Hilson's table. Hilson was an English teacher who spent faculty meetings playing rounds of "Blame the Teacher," his personal version of bingo. Whenever the principal or an administrator pointed the finger at teachers for why kids were failing, Hilson added a chip to his card. It usually took him only a few minutes to win a round. On a good day he could clear two or three cards in one meeting. A graduate of the University of California, Los Angeles, and a film buff, he had attended Aviation as a child about twenty-five years earlier. He lived five minutes from the school with his wife, also a teacher, and their two school-age kids, neither of whom attended Aviation. Instead they were bused ten miles to a public school on the west side—the white side—of LA. Hilson laid out his table's problem.

Forty-two percent of students in the seventh grade scored below passing on the state test . . . Why is that?

1. Students are socially promoted, even without mastery of grade-level standards . . . Why is that?
2. Retaining kids is problematic . . . Why is that?
3. We don't have the infrastructure to support students who are falling behind or who are multiple grade levels behind . . . Why is that?
4. The people in power have mixed motives and thus will not own the real problem . . . Why is that?
5. Forget it, Jake. It's Chinatown.

A funhouse of trapdoors and two-way mirrors with the instructions for escape written in disappearing ink.

In my mother's favorite book from childhood, *Wings for Per*—about the young boy who fled war and vowed to return to set his people free—the narrator tells us: "The next day [Per] stood behind the ruins of his school when enemy soldiers marched the teacher and the parson away . . . 'First the enemy took our food, and now they have taken our teachers.'" In that fictional account, invading enemies went after a nation's teachers because they knew that teachers are as essential to the life of a people as food is to the body or a parson is to the soul. This is no longer seen as knowledge, not in this nation. But a people that pillories its teachers imperils itself. That is true for every nation.

11

Super Sub

Ethan had had it with Shayla. She plainly held the monopoly of power at Cullen. The administrators were eager for her to like them. She'd flatter them by complimenting their hair or shoes and they were convinced it gave them an in with her. But she had them snowed. She and Ethan would end up in the admin office for another round of reconnection—the let's-bury-the-hatchet-and-work-things-out meeting they required of teachers and students anytime a student got sent out—and Shayla would turn to Ethan and say, "When this dumb bitch comes in here, we're gonna say what we gotta say, but I'm still gonna hate your ass."

Ethan was almost on Shayla's side on that score. The administration was ridiculous, playing to the fifteen-, sixteen-, and seventeen-year-old "clients" they were supposed to be in charge of. The assistant principal had blown up at Ethan for sending students out after he had made the mistake of meeting with her alone. Every time after that, he met her with his union rep. But he didn't want to get entangled with a union fight; he just wanted peace and quiet in his classroom so he could teach.

More than anything he wanted to get his kids prepared for the

California High School Exit Examination (CAHSEE). He'd made such strides with them as they eventually responded to his expectations. He had a method. Whatever the steps were to solve a problem, he had the students write them out on the first day of a lesson, then he had them recite the steps out loud every time he put a sample problem on the board. This was Ethan using his outer voice to make them use their outer voice, until it was a part of their inner voice and the steps would come to their mind without being prompted or needing to hear it out loud. He color-coded problems on each slide, from easiest to hardest, insisting that every student do at least one of the problems on the board: "Do the hardest one you understand." That way everyone had a sense of accomplishment while also being challenged. And, more important, it helped him figure out who needed help and who was doing fine.

The practice exams plainly showed that the students' scores were improving. His mentor, Ms. Bernard, the thirty-year veteran science teacher from LSU with the gold-tinged locks, who lived not far from the school and had seen it at its best and its worst, had poked her head in one day to tell Ethan she'd heard he was doing good things. And the sense of accomplishment his kids got when they aced a test told him the same thing.

But fifth period was still at the mercy of Shayla, and he could not get her to yield. Some days she could be so charming, but others, when she was frustrated or angry and got everyone in the class riled up, were a lost cause. He could feel the kids teetering on the edge. By December nearly all of his other classes had gotten with the program. The kids knew how important the CAHSEE was, and the ones who didn't either didn't come to class or got themselves put out. But those numbers were dwindling. A failed CAHSEE meant no diploma, and nearly all of them wanted it. Ethan had sworn to them he'd get them to pass if they just did what he needed them to do.

Late in January, with two months to go before the CAHSEE,

Shayla flipped on Ethan, calling him every possible name in the book and he, as he always did when kids cursed him, kicked her out. He'd had enough. Even with her gone, he could barely refocus. He was angry, frustrated, and spent. He refused yet another reconnection meeting with administration because they were a waste of time. He decided he'd try Ms. Bernard instead. She and Shayla seemed to have a good rapport. He went up to her class on the third floor to ask her if she'd mediate between him and Shayla, and she agreed. Ms. Bernard was probably not much older than fifty, but she was good and wise. She had grown up in the neighborhood of Watts, as had her mother and grandmother. She knew Cullen when it had been a quality place to send your kids.

At the end of sixth period, Ethan ducked out of his class to head to Ms. Bernard's classroom. She'd sent for Shayla without telling her why. When Shayla entered the room and saw Ethan sitting there, she said, "Oh, hell naw!" and turned on her heels. "Shayla!" Ms. Bernard barked at her, positioning her voice on the line between command and request. Then, more softly: "Have a seat, please." Shayla sat, grumpily, her arms crossed and face clenched in disgust.

"So, Shayla," Ms. Bernard began. "Mr. Adshade came to me to ask me to mediate between the two of you. The two of you have been going back and forth all year. And something's gotta give. So what I'm gonna do is I'm gonna let you talk. Let you explain what's been going on. And why you're having such a difficult time respecting his class and respecting his rules."

"Because he is a bitch ass," Shayla replied. Ms. Bernard was unfazed.

"Okay, but I'm gonna need more than that."

"Ain't no more than that! He gets on my fuckin' nerves and everybody the fuck else's. I'm sick of his shit."

"Okay, Shayla, I see. So why don't you tell me what's really going on?"

"Ain't nothing going on! I told you. I'm sick of his bullshit. He think he better than everybody else."

"No, I—" Ethan began, but Ms. Bernard raised her hand, silencing him. He was a bit confused by what was going on. Ms. Bernard was not one to let students curse around her, but she was letting Shayla vent. Ethan stayed quiet.

"Okay, so like I said, why don't you tell me what's really going on?"

"He the fuck what's going on! He a whack-ass teacher and don't no the fuck body understand his white ass! I ain't the only one either. Don't nobody like his stupid ass."

"Okay, I hear you, but what's really going on?"

"He the fuck what's going on! He fucking get on my damn nerves. He always in my face, talking stupid shit. But I don't give a fuck about his stupid-ass class."

Ms. Bernard listened, then asked Shayla again, "So what's really going on?"

Shayla began to blink furiously. "I'm tired of him. I'm tired of this fucking school. Everybody always coming for me. And I'm sick of it. That's what."

Ms. Bernard nodded, then said, " Okay Shayla, but I'm waiting for you to tell me what's really going on with you."

By this time Shayla was crying. She just shook her head. No words. Ms. Bernard waited but the tears kept coming. Finally, "I don't want my mom to come back."

Ms. Bernard nodded. "What do you mean?"

"She just got out of prison and she trying to come back in my life and I don't want nothing to do with her. I just want her to leave me alone."

Shayla continued sobbing. She'd been born in prison to a mother who she now wanted nothing to do with. She was happier that way. And now her mother's release threatened to make a difficult life even worse. That is what was going on. "I didn't know," Ethan offered.

Shayla turned to Ethan. "I don't mean to be such a bitch all the time. I just got a lot I'm dealing with and I'm sorry. I see you trying to help us. I just feel like I don't have nobody out there for me except my granny."

Ethan finally spoke. "But I pray for you, Shayla," he said. "I pray for you every day." Why he said it out loud he didn't know, but it was true.

Shayla fell silent and dropped her head, tears raining into her lap.

Ms. Bernard rubbed a motherly hand on Shayla's back and said, "Go wipe your face, sweetheart. There's tissues on my desk."

Shayla walked to the desk as Bernard leaned over to Ethan. "I think we should pray right now," she whispered. "Would that be okay with you?"

Would it be okay? A man who'd grown up with a father who could be found standing in the middle of his room in the wee hours of the morning, raising his arms to heaven, overcome with the Holy Spirit? Who took him into the poorest areas of Miami armed with clothes and food to give away because God had called him to, despite the fact that the meager wages he earned as a tree cutter meant his family subsisted just barely above the poverty line during the winters when work was scarce? Would he be okay with praying? Ethan nodded yes.

Shayla crossed back from the desk, wiping her face. Ms. Bernard asked her, "Shayla, I'm thinking about us praying right now. Would you be okay with that?" Shayla smiled through her tears and nodded yes. She sat back down and the three of them—the white surfer kid from Florida who'd never planned on being a teacher in the first place but now knew that education was his calling; the science teacher with the gold-tinged locks who'd never abandoned her neighborhood even during its darkest days; and Shayla, the sixteen-year-old sophomore who had been born in Twin Towers prison to a mother she wanted nothing to do with

and a father she never knew—joined hands on the third floor of
Countee Cullen High School, just west of Interstate 110, in the
heart of Watts, bowed their heads together, and they prayed.

By the start of the third week of the second semester, I'd sent Erik
out of my classroom eight times. Sometimes alone, sometimes with
two of his friends. He wasn't the only asshole in that class. After
the assistant principal of Little Cullen called me into his office and
saw that I wasn't budging on this issue, he relented and we came
up with a solution. Erik would do his work in another classroom.
He could stay for the lesson, so long as he was listening and paying attention, but once classwork started, he'd have to do his work
in another teacher's classroom. I just had to find a willing teacher.
Luckily a young long-term sub had started working there too, and
she boasted that she and Erik got along fine. She had been able to
win him over and thus seemed amusingly perplexed by the hub-
bub. For the record, no teacher likes teachers like that. If you get
along with a student who treats every other teacher like shit, keep
it to yourself. No one cares to hear you humble-brag that you're the
asshole whisperer. And when the asshole you've been whispering to
eventually calls you a stupid bitch like Erik did this young sub halfway through the semester, the other teachers will dance a mental jig.

So Erik was out of the picture, although his friends still gave
me the flux. But they too got sent out of the room. I was most concerned about Rodiney. He had moved out of honors classes and the
break with Greg and Dayshawn seemed to have been a real body
blow. But time didn't heal the wound. Rodiney was getting worse.
And other teachers remarked that he had become essentially
despondent in their classes too.

One day in class, before Erik left for the other teacher's classroom, he was sitting behind Rodiney, who had his head down. I
was busy trying to work through one concept or another but my
peripheral vision told me that something was going on. Erik was

quiet but laughing. His buddies too. Not loud enough to justify ejecting them in the middle of the lesson, so I let it be. Then, as I was finishing up the slide presentation, I heard a thin, desperate, pained yelp. It was Rodiney. He shot up from his seat, his school bag in hand, knocked his desk over, and ran out.

Erik and his buddies seemed partly amused, partly perplexed. But in that moment I knew, without knowing why, that Rodiney was being bullied. I tried to talk to Rodiney, but, still stuck in his daze, he wouldn't tell me anything. I asked his other teachers, but they knew nothing. I scanned the halls between classes trying to find evidence of what I knew to be true. I kept Erik and his pals completely separated in my class and sent Erik out the minute he raised a quarrelsome eyebrow, even if my lesson wasn't over. Once, during the change of classes, I saw Rodiney in the hall, hugging the far wall, as Erik walked down the center of the hall in the other direction. Erik spat something at Rodiney with a grin, but Rodiney kept his eyes straight ahead.

Lunch was the only time Rodiney seemed to experience any measure of joy, playing soccer with the ninth-graders. You could actually see something approaching a smile on his face. But that didn't last. I wasn't at school the day it came to a head. As I heard the story, Rodiney was playing soccer during lunch. He had possession and was close to the goal when the bell for fifth period was about to sound. As he neared the orange cones that served as the goal, he struck for the game-winning point, but the ball went just wide of the cones. He was crushed. Erik, who had been watching from the side of the field, was laughing and pointing, mocking Rodiney mercilessly. Something in Rodiney collapsed. He ran into the office and said, "The devil is telling me to kill myself." That afternoon the assistant principal left a message on my phone, telling me what had happened and asking if I'd be at school the next day. Apparently, Rodiney had asked him to call me. When his mother and stepfather came to school the next day, I spoke with them. The assistant principal had already called the district psychiatrist, but Rodiney's mother was resisting dealing with her. Rodiney's mother felt that this was a spiritual matter. That as long as "that boy" (Erik) left her son alone, she could deal with Rodiney's problems on her own. I did not want to offend her, so I told her I was the son of a preacher and agreed that surely his struggles had a spiritual component, but medicine could help. "God made doctors too."

I left that conversation worried that his parents would not make the right choice for Rodiney. The mother continued to speak with the assistant principal as I went into the hall. The stepfather followed me and asked for my number. They were going to take Rodiney out of school for a few days and thought that it might do some good if he could still be in contact with me while he was out. The stepfather also said he had a sister with mental illness and that the medication the doctors prescribed helped her get her life together; he would work on bringing his wife around. I saw the concern in his face and wondered if I'd judged him too harshly when I'd first met him in Mr. Titus's office. There was a more responsible side to him and I was happy to see it emerge just as his son needed it. I spoke to Rodiney on the phone twice while he was out. He asked if I thought he should take medication. His voice was so small that I struggled to hear him. I told him I thought it would help. I repeated what I had told his mother: "God made doctors too."

A week later Rodiney came back to school, but he was not visibly better. Rodiney's face had the telltale signs of someone on psychotropic drugs. But he apparently wanted to come back to school. I let him keep his head down. Erik could no longer be in any class with him, so Erik did his work either in the office (when he came to school) or in another teacher's class. I prodded Rodiney about his work as gently as I could. He attempted things here and there, but for the most part he was as distant and unreachable as he had been before. I spoke with the district psychologists and his stepfather about adjusting his meds, and both seemed to believe it would take some time but eventually the drugs would even out to his benefit. Rodiney's stepfather, who turned out to be a serious man, had seen it with his sister. I let it rest and just encouraged Rodiney. I let him stay in my classroom during lunch and the fifteen-minute break in the morning. His head never moved from the desk.

Rodiney's suffering cast a pall over me that I couldn't really shake. But I tried to refocus on my other duties. As spring break approached and my students prepared to take their CAHSEE exams, I was more focused on helping my one class of seniors who hadn't yet passed the test. I had a basic vocabulary exercise to help them with word recognition that seemed to be working. The tenth-graders were feeling stressed too, so I took some time out of history class to help them study. I tried to discuss with the assistant principal what to do about Rodiney. When we asked him if he wanted to take the CAHSEE, he just shrugged and barely lifted his head from the desk.

At one point, a week before the test, Mr. Titus came to my door and asked if I'd be available to sub the day after spring break. They'd mercifully found a permanent teacher to take over the history class once spring break was over, but he wanted to know if I was still available to work. I wasn't sure but I gave him a tentative yes, even though I was exhausted and wanted nothing else to do with school, any school, for a while. Apparently Clarice overheard the conversation.

"Why they always asking you to sub for people?"

I shrugged and said, "Because I'm good at it and I'm not scared of y'all."

But she had made up her mind to try to bug me. "Look—who's that flying in the sky? It's Super Sub." I gave her a quizzical look. I sensed the potential danger of where she was headed. I wanted to stop her but it was too late.

"What? Ms. Jackson is sick tomorrow? And you need me to sub? Don't fear: Super Sub is here!" A smattering of laughter from the kids. It wasn't the funniest joke, but the look in her eyes told me she knew what I knew: that she was onto something here. Clarice was a true comedian and she could sense when something had legs. Everything inside me said, *You're in trouble here. She's got a bead on you.* My natural instinct was to kill this beast in its cradle, to try to talk over her or drum up some outrage, but any hope I had of killing it died after she reached into her book bag, pulled out her cellphone, and pretended to talk into it. Yeah, she was fully committing to this.

"What's that?" she said into the phone. "Mr. Valenzuela's car broke down? It's not sitting on dubs?* This a job for Super Sub!" More laughter. The joke was getting a little better. Now she was standing, really going for it. I was being murdered.

She moved the phone to her other ear. "What's that you say? Ms. Williams can't make it? You need me to watch her class? I'm Super Sub and I'm on that ass."

I couldn't even be angry that she'd cussed, because I know the rules. When a talented, good-natured comedian is roasting you alive, especially a sixteen-year-old one, you let her have the floor. She had a right to the monopoly of power at that moment, because wit and intelligence got her there, not force and anger. I played my part, with mock outrage that acknowledged my respect and a half-suppressed urge to laugh. But what I was really saying was, "Keep standing. Keep doing this. Keep the fun and comity and goodwill

---

* Dubs = W's, as in *wheels*.

flowing, even at my complete expense. I'll be the sacrificial lamb and take it on the chin. This is all for the greater good."

On she went as the class laughed louder and louder. And then, suddenly, she whipped around at me and barked, "Wait!" She stopped her routine cold, no longer in character. The laughter was gone from her face and just as quickly the other students in the room sat spellbound, watching her and wondering what was coming next. Clarice stood silently in the middle of the room. Her face was so calm as she peered at me that I almost felt like I was in danger. She tilted her head to the side and, in as serious a tone as she could manage, asked, "Do you sleep in your clothes? So you can already be dressed when they call you in the morning?" And with that, sixth-period World History at Countee Cullen was over for the day. The laughter was so loud I could feel waves of the sound. All I could do was shake my head at her and mouth softly, "Sit down, Clarice." She shrugged and sat down to geysers of joy.

After that day I could hear kids yelling, "It's a bird! It's a plane! It's SUPER SUUUUUB!!!" as I walked down the hall. I admit, it was less than ideal. But great black comedy always has a little bite. And being called "Super Sub" for the remainder of my days at Cullen was an acceptable price to pay, because as Clarice's routine wound up, I glanced over to the corner of the room to see Rodiney staring at Clarice. His mouth was open and looked warped, almost like it had been hastily pasted onto the bottom of his face. It was as if his brain was sending signals to his mouth to smile, but only part of the message was getting through. Three bursts of air came from his throat, like someone firing a gun. The signal was laughter, and part of that message was not delivered either. But it didn't matter. Rodiney's brain had been slowly finding the levels it needed to return him to a recognizable version of himself, and I saw a glimmer of it as I was being roasted alive. He was coming back to himself, enjoying one of the greatest pleasures a child ever experiences: watching the adult in charge getting hilariously eaten alive by one of their own. That day, Clarice, purest of knuckleheads, helped bring Rodiney back from the brink. I could live with being Super Sub for the rest of the year.

12

Final Days

The end of the school year approached. Cullen was both more set-tled and more restless. A good 15 to 20 percent of the student body had dropped out—some were lovely kids, others not so much. The students who remained were by and large the ones serious about getting their diplomas or too afraid of their parents not to try. After spring break I took time off for a few more weeks. Eventually Cullen called to ask if I'd be willing to sub for the last week of school. I hadn't seen the students in almost two months, and I was curious how everyone was. Clarice was still the undisputed Connect Four champion and still hysterically funny. When I saw her that first day back, she looked at me angrily and barked, "Where you been?!"

I smiled at her warmly. "Hey, Clarice, it's nice to see you." She rolled her eyes and mumbled, "Whatever." Clarice had missed me, and that was her way of saying it.

I had called Rodiney's stepfather a few times but he never re-turned my calls. Greg and Dayshawn were still doing fine, excited about summer vacation. Junior had a girlfriend and, well, it calmed him and his hormones down. David, aka Dr. Sleep, had a job lined up at Fat Burger but his parents wouldn't let him start until school was out. And Rodiney had found some equilibrium. He wasn't hanging with Greg and Dayshawn like he had before, but their freeze seemed to have thawed. And Erik was gone. Mercifully. From what I learned, he had been taunting a ninth-grader who happened to be the cousin of a black guy who rolled with David and liked to fight. His name was Rolando, and he was as quiet and pleasant a kid as you'd ever meet. But he had heard Erik was taunting his cousin, and one day he surged up behind David and clocked Erik right in the mouth, knocking him on his back. It was the talk of the school for weeks. Erik didn't show up much after that and eventually dropped out. School, in other words, was continuing as normal.

The CAHSEE results were in, too. Of the five seniors I had coached, four took the exam (one kid didn't show up), and three passed. They'd remembered to read the test question first, then go back and read the prompt. They tackled the easiest questions, then the hard ones. And they recognized all the vocabulary words! Easy points.

But the scores of Ethan Adshade's students were great. A full 80 percent of his students passed the math portion of the CAHSEE, an improvement of nearly 15 percent. Even Shayla passed.

One day at lunch there was a knock on my door. It was Rodiney, and his girlfriend was with him. A freshman. Pretty, sweet. I'd taught her once, but didn't know her. He asked if they could both eat in my class during lunch. I said they could. They sat and listened to music and talked while I watched YouTube videos. Right before the bell was about to ring, they headed out. I exchanged a few pleasantries with Rodiney, and then he asked: "You gonna be here next year, Mister?"

I lied. "Maybe."

"Oh, okay, cool." I asked him what he'd done over spring break.

"I just chilled," he said. As he and his girlfriend reached the door, I told him to tell his mom and dad hello for me. He said he would, and then he offered, "You oughta be a real teacher, Mister." His girlfriend—whom I'd only taught once—nodded.

"Yeah," he said. "You could teach the history class again." I'd heard rumors that the students didn't like the new history teacher the school hired, but I wasn't about to dig into why.

I looked at him quizzically. There was no chance of me becoming a "real" teacher. I simply said, "What? And deal with you knuckleheads all day?"

They laughed. "Yeah, true," he replied, and they headed into the hall.

On the last day of school I was moved from room to room as the administration needed me. The assistant principal asked me what I was planning to do next year. He knew I was a writer, and I told him I had a cool job lined up. "We could use some more black men in teaching, Henderson," he offered. I demurred. A few students asked that week if I was going to be around next year and I deflected. I'd taught every kid in the school by then and knew a good many of them well. I was going to miss quite a few of them; that was for sure.

I was heading out of the teacher's lounge when a teacher, Ms. Brattle, caught up to me and asked if I could watch her sixth period. She'd forgotten about a meeting at a sister campus and couldn't get a sub. She told me she'd left some simple work for the class to do. I was floating that day anyway, so I said sure.

As I headed to her classroom, I passed the assistant principal in the hall, who told me to check my email. The bell rang, and Ms. Brattle's kids settled in quietly. I passed out crossword puzzles, pens, and markers—last-day-of-school kind of work, and they chatted and drew or played on their phones. I considered all the things I'd seen and done that year. About ten thousand students, more than fifty different schools—it was a lot to think about, and in some way I was wistful that it was coming to an end. I was gonna miss that place. I had helped some kids, and plenty of kids needed a lot more. I also was surprised to learn that I knew how to teach, to explain difficult things to young people so that they understood. And that I really, deeply enjoyed it. And that when it's good, it's great. But when it goes badly, it is heartbreakingly bad.

Thinking about all the students I'd encountered during that year in Los Angeles and all the teachers, I marveled at how different education had become since even I was a kid, and since even older generations had peopled the societies of the world. What, in its humblest state, saw Plato explaining the most complex ideas in the open-air markets of ancient Greece without so much as a book or chalkboard, or saw refugees from one conflict or another learning in open-air tents in their adopted country was now, in contemporary times, a multibillion-dollar professional industry thick with arcana and fancy titles and jargon all its own. But didn't the Greeks teach Greek to their children without computers and advanced degrees? Didn't they teach them how to paint and sculpt and read and think? Didn't the Xhosa teach their children to speak Xhosa without computers and fancy theories about how to teach them to speak it? Surely it was, at least in part, the fanciness and the delight in fanciness that helped lead us astray.

We manage to forget that human beings have been teaching their young since the beginning of time. That ours is not the first society to confront poverty or brutal oppression. But teaching goes on nonetheless. I recall watching a close friend teach a ballet class. As she counted through first position, second position, third, fourth, and fifth, all her charges shifted and stretched their arms and feet at her command. I realized, with a sudden sense of awe, that the five positions are as old as the modern world. The clutch of young students in South LA was rehearsing the same movements that have been done for nearly four centuries. Diaghilev, Nijinsky, Fokin, Petipa, and Nureyev did them. Baryshnikov did them. Anna Pavlova and Margot Fonteyn and Martha Graham did them. Alvin Ailey and Judith Jamison. Arthur Mitchell and Alicia Alonso and

Raven Wilkinson. Over and over and over and over until they did them without thinking. And each stood quietly and patiently before the teacher who corrected them, sometimes kindly, sometimes harshly, when they got a position wrong. Even when they groused inside or felt tired or angry or were convinced the teacher hated them, they formed these positions, patiently and repeatedly, until they were masters of movement themselves.

It is not the job of teachers and educators to move as quickly as the world around them or as quickly as students want them to. Barack Obama, bemoaning the speed at which he had to make decisions as president, once said, "The most important thing you need to do is to have big chunks of time during the day when all you're doing is thinking." A teacher's job is to carve out that time, to slow students down, to get them to stop and think, to shut off their phones and close their mouths and leave the baggage of the rest of their lives at the door. Our responsibility to students is to sometimes bore them to tears but show them that working through boredom with the same grit they work through something that fascinates them is the key to the future we wish for them. The *only* key to the future we wish for them. The role of teachers in every society, in every time, is to slowly forge that key, to point children to the door it opens, to push wide that door and set the child free to run through it. For a teacher that is all there is.

I was deep in my daydream when I suddenly heard someone yell, "What the hell?" Before I could fully register it or speak up, a student said: "Girl, watch your mouth!" "Sorry, Mr. Henderson." It was Sierra. I nodded without even looking over. By then she knew how I felt about cursing; they all did. They went back to their teenage talk. An email came through on my computer. It was from the assistant principal, who had forwarded a link from Western Governors University, where he got his master's in teaching. It's all online: eighteen months, no books to lug around, no classroom. A go-at-your-own-pace kinda thing. Designed for people with full lives. "You could go to school and do your other job, too," he wrote. That sounded impossible. But he would get fifty bucks off if I listened to an introductory seminar. I started filling out the form. Couldn't hurt to hear the people out, right?

But before I could finish and hit Send, I heard, "I can't wait to get home. I'm gonna get me some d-i-c-c." It took me a minute. It was Sierra again. I slowly looked up from the computer. *Did she say what I think she just said?* I looked over at her and stared for a second. Did she just misspell the word *dick*? From the way she was moaning and groaning and writhing in her seat, I was pretty sure that's what she'd done. *Jesus, What now? She was trying to be respectful, spelling the word instead of saying it, but how do I tell her I don't need to hear her misspelling* dick *in my class? What if she asks me the right spelling? And she* will *ask.* The last thing I needed was for the assistant principal to walk in as I was at the whiteboard conducting this particular English lesson. Sierra's friend Randall was gay and from the way he was moaning and groaning, maybe he was unsure of the spelling too. By then both were moaning and groaning, dreaming about d-i-c-c. What the hell was I gonna do? Watching them in all their teenage glory, I suddenly started laughing to myself. I struggled to contain it, but they eventually saw me shaking in my chair. They wanted to know what was so funny, but I waved them off. By then, I was wiping away tears because I was laughing so hard. After nearly a year of working in more than fifty schools attended by thousands of kids, most of them wonderful, some of them jerks, facing some type of challenge nearly every day I stood in front of a group of kids I'd never seen before and many times would never see again, on my very last day as a substitute teacher, it all came down to Sierra and Randall dreaming about *d-i-c-c.* I managed, through tears, to complete the teacher application form and hit Send. I guess, I'd give this school a listen. I mean, how could anyone not miss this place?

WHAT CAN WE DO NOW?

Teach impulse control. Students from Kentucky to California should be trained in impulse control from their first days in school. Studies show it can be done by supplementing the too-often-inadequate efforts at socializing children so they will thrive and help others to thrive. Start socialization early and redouble the efforts at the middle-school level when hormones (and cursing) kick in. (A warning: A school's teachers should decide whether its students need training in impulse control. A principal will pretend the school has no such problem.)

No more charter schools. The school choice movement has been a boondoggle for the rich and there is no chance of improving our nation's struggling schools if one tiny charter school after another is allowed to compete for the narrowest number of public funds. Schools need economies of scale to be outfitted with the kind of co-curricular amenities that give life to a school. School leaders cannot be panicked that losing ten kids over a semester will mean firing a teacher at the end of the year.

Channel private donations directly to poor schools. In California and most states, schools receive a large portion of their funding from property taxes. In economically depressed areas, that amounts to next to nothing. But, depending on the state, there are regulations on giving private donations directly to schools. If smaller, failing charters schools can be reconstituted back into robust, larger ones, the charter school philanthropists can redirect their largesse directly to the poor public school districts to make up for shortfalls in teacher salaries, Latin classes, band classes, home ec and shop classes, bringing them financially on par with schools in wealthier neighborhoods. Philanthropists can also spearhead the funding of the newly constituted reform schools, which I mention below.

Bring back reform schools . . . and reform them. Reform schools should be easy to get into and easy to get out of, and charter schools can compete to innovate to administer to the most troubled youth. Throw the light of day on these alternative schools so that the best and wisest practitioners are the ones in charge. They should be designed to give struggling kids the third and fourth chances as well as the holistic, reparative therapy and counseling they need, in addition to stringency, consequences, expectations, and opportunities to repair the mistakes they've made. Robust alternative schools give expelled or suspended students some place to go other than the streets.

Reinstate classroom ejections, suspensions, and expulsions. Without the power to remove a student from a class momentarily, from a school temporarily, or from a school environment permanently, adults in schools have no power at all.

Hire more black men to teach. The absence of fathers has had a devastating effect on the development of black boys. Black male teachers can be powerful surrogates, but efforts to recruit more of them have been unsuccessful. Billionaire philanthropists can set up a fund to pay down the college debt of black male college graduates who go into teaching in black schools for five years or more, especially in middle schools where they are most needed. And

Barack Obama should lead the way, teaching government part time at a high school in Washington, DC.

Make middle schools the most important schools. Every problem of student achievement and behavior emerges in earnest in middle school. All the money and attention of governments, nonprofits, school boards, and parents should be focused on creating strong, structured, disciplined middle schools with empowered, authoritative teachers at the head of every class.

Bring back (limited) tracks. Though I have not discussed this in the previous pages, I found consistently that there were no intellectual stereotypes separating the type of Latino immigrant kids and poor black kids who went to school together in LA. The ancient stereotypes about intelligence that divided black and white (and Asian) kids never seemed to inhere in mixed black and Latino schools. I recognize this is a point with many implications that I cannot adequately explore here, but I know of no teacher who genuinely felt that they could successfully teach kids who all had drastically different achievement levels. Reinstituting limited tracks in certain schools can give teachers the opportunity to tailor their instruction to students' real needs while avoiding problem behavior caused by boredom or confusion.

Crack down on cursing. Students should be free to say to each other in private whatever they want, but cursing within earshot of an adult in a school should not be allowed, especially in middle schools. The punishment should not be extreme (though cursing at a teacher should get you sent home for the day).

Use the courts. The one valuable innovation of charter schools has been to demonstrate the importance of parental participation in the running of a school. If we cannot begin a serious and consequential debate about the obligation parents have to cooperate with teachers and administrators, then students and parents should sue school districts to compel rules around some basic level of parental involvement (a few hours every semester maybe). Legislatures can devise new legal obligations for parents, who should be subjected to reasonable consequences if they fail to meet those baseline obligations. This is a serious philosophical question: What does a citizen owe the state and community in exchange for government-funded education for their child?

NOTES

INTRODUCTION

1. "Profile of ClassDojo Founders Sam Chaudhary and Liam Don," interview by Sara Mead, *Education Week*, June 11, 2013, http://blogs.edweek.org/edweek/sarameads_policy_notebook/2013/06/sam_chaudhary_and_liam_don_co-founders_classdojo.html.
2. J. D. Vance, *Hillbilly Elegy* (New York: HarperCollins, 2016), 127.
3. Emily Badger, Claire Cain Miller, Adam Pearce, and Kevin Quealy, "Extensive Data Shows Punishing Reach of Racism for Black Boys," The Upshot (blog), *The New York Times*, March 19, 2018, https://www.nytimes.com/interactive/2018/03/19/upshot/race-class-white-and-black-men.html?mtrref=www.google.com.

1. KIDS' RIGHTS, OR BY ALL MEANS VOTE FOR THAT IDIOT!

1. "Summerhill: The Early Years," A. S. Neill's Summerhill, n.d., http://www.summerhillschool.co.uk/history.php.
2. Jonathan Croall, *Neill of Summerhill: The Permanent Rebel* (New York: Pantheon Books, 1983), 55, 76.
3. Paul Goodman, "Reflections on Children's Rights," in *The Children's Rights Movement: Overcoming the Oppression of Young People*, ed. Beatrice Gross and Paul Gross (New York: Anchor, 1977), 141–42.

4. Karen Attiah, "Why Won't the U.S. Ratify the U.N.'s Child Rights Treaty?" *The Washington Post*, November 21, 2014, https://www.washingtonpost.com/blogs/post-partisan/wp/2014/11/21/why-wont-the-u-s-ratify-the-u-n-s-child-rights-treaty/?utm_term=.63fcc20b0417.

5. Martha Minow, "Whatever Happened to Children's Rights?" *Minnesota Law Review* 80, no. 2 (1995): 267–298.

6. Steven Levitt and Stephen J. Dubner, *Freakonomics* (New York: Harper Collins, 2005), 103; Michelle Alexander, *The New Jim Crow* (New York: The New Press, 2010), 51. For "Four Horsemen of the Apocalypse," Alexander quotes David Kennedy's *Don't Shoot: One Man, a Street Fellowship, and the End of Violence in the Inner City* (New York: Bloomsbury, 2011), 10.

7. Levitt and Dubner, *Freakonomics*. Zero tolerance is a policy term of art that has both an official government meaning and an ad hoc localized meaning. I refer to both here. The government usage refers to the Gun-Free School Zone Act enacted by the Clinton administration in 1990 that forced states to expel students who brought guns to school. Individual schools and school districts also enacted their own local zero tolerance policies for a wider number of offenses, everything from fighting to selling candy on campus without permission.

8. "Jay-Z: The Fresh Air Interview," interview by Terry Gross, NPR, originally broadcast November 16, 2010, https://www.npr.org/2017/06/16/533216823/jay-z-the-fresh-air-interview.

9. Shawn Carter, *Decoded* (New York: Spiegel & Grau, 2010), 12.

10. Ibid., 13.

11. Jacob V. Lamar, "Kids Who Sell Crack," *Time*, June 24, 2001, http://content.time.com/time/magazine/article/0,9171,149199,00.html.

12. Carter, *Decoded*, 13.

13. Eleonore Marchand, "Christy Conquers All," *Harper's Bazaar Australia*, April 2017, https://archive.org/stream/14mar23/14mar23_djvu.txt.

14. Martin Palmer, "Jada Pinkett Smith: A True Force of Will," *Daily Mail*, October 6, 2012, http://www.dailymail.co.uk/home/you/article-2211784/Jada-true-force-Will.html.

2. BROKEN WINDOWS

1. The controversial concept of broken windows policing was promulgated by James Q. Wilson, then a professor of government at Harvard, and George L. Kelling, a criminologist who is now a senior fellow at the Manhattan Institute for Public Policy, to describe the crime epidemic of

the 1980s. Briefly, they argued that if a window is broken and left unrepaired, people walking by will conclude that no one cares and no one is in charge, providing an open invitation to greater criminality. Repair the window and punish the breaker, the reasoning went, and you'd deter tougher criminals from coming around, because they'd know even minor lawlessness was not allowed. The police tactics that grew out of this are widely held to have led to the overcriminalization of the penal system. See James Q. Wilson and George L. Kelling, "Broken Windows: The Police and Neighborhood Safety," *The Atlantic*, March 1982, https://www.theatlantic.com/magazine/archive/1982/03/broken-windows/304465/.

2. Yudhijit Bhattacharjee, "Why We Lie: The Science Behind Our Deceptive Ways," *National Geographic*, June 2017, https://www.nationalgeographic.com/magazine/2017/06/lying-hoax-false-fibs-science/. The connection between cursing and lying is more than suggestive, as Steven Pinker, a psychologist and language expert, implies: "Swearing and hypocrisy go hand in hand, to the extent that some personality questionnaires included items like 'I sometimes swear' as a check for lying." Steven Pinker, *The Stuff of Thought* (New York: Viking, 2007), 330.

3. Pinker, *The Stuff of Thought*, 333.

4. "Reminding Me," featuring Chantay Savage, track 16 on Common, *One Day It'll All Make Sense*, Relativity Records, 1997.

5. Kate Wiles, "Swearing: The Fascinating History of Our Favorite Four-Letter Words," *The New Republic*, February 22, 2014, https://newrepublic.com/article/116713/swear-word-history-where-your-favorite-curses-came.

6. Louise Greenspan and Julia Deardorff, *The New Puberty* (New York: Rodale, 2014), xii; "Black Boys Entering Puberty Earlier Than Counterparts," *The Chronicle* (Winston-Salem), November 1, 2012, http://www.wschronicle.com/2012/11/black-boys-entering-puberty-earlier-than-counterparts/.

7. David F. Lancy, *The Anthropology of Childhood* (Cambridge: Cambridge University Press, 2015), 22.

3. GEMS, KNUCKLEHEADS, AND ASSHOLES

1. Paul Tough, *Helping Children Succeed* (New York: Houghton Mifflin, 2016), 89.

2. Peter Wallsten, "Michelle Obama Confronts Protester, Threatens to Leave Fundraiser," *The Washington Post*, June 4, 2013, https://www.washingtonpost

.com/news/post-politics/wp/2013/06/04/michelle-obama-confronts -protester-threatens-to-leave-fundraiser/?utm_term=.c41b19e3b24a; Amber Phillips, "Obama to White House Heckler: You're in My House," *The Washington Post*, June 25, 2015, https://www.washingtonpost.com /news/the-fix/wp/2015/06/25/obama-to-white-house-heckler-youre-in -my-house-but-is-it/?utm_term=.ec7226eebc67; Spencer Buell, "Barack Obama Super-Secret Speech Leaks," *Boston Magazine*, February 27, 2018; *Inside Out*, dir. Peter Docter and Ronnie Del Carmen, Pixar Studios, 2015; *Moonlight*, dir. Barry Jenkins, A24 Studios, 2017.

3. Richard Wolf, "Protest on Campaign Spending Disrupts Supreme Court," *USA Today*, January 21, 2015.

4. Joseph Goldstein, "A Cigarette for 75c, 2 for $1: The Brisk Shady Sales of Loosies," *The New York Times*, April 4, 2011.

5. Paul Tough, *How Children Succeed* (New York: Houghton Mifflin, 2012), 106–107, 127, 128.

6. "About Us," Liahona Treatment Center, https://www.liahonaacademy .com/about-us.html; Gregory Kane, "Pa. Reform School Keeps Kids on Right Path," *The Baltimore Sun*, March 6, 2002, http://articles.baltimore sun.com/2002-03-06/news/0203060062_1_glen-mills-reform-school -residence-halls.

4. A CANDID WORLD

1. The work of Danielle Allen has been highly instructive for me in this chapter. Her essay "What Is Education For?" lays out the case for civic agency. *Boston Review*, May 2016, http://bostonreview.net/forum/danielle -allen-what-education.

2. I borrow this idea from Danielle Allen's remarkable book, *Our Declaration: A Reading of the Declaration of Independence in Defense of Equality* (New York: Liveright Books, 2014).

3. Again, as I was formulating this idea of preparing children for a fight, I was not surprised to find that Danielle Allen had gotten there before me, though she defines the idea of "fair fighting" differently. See her *Boston Review* essay, "What Is Education For?"

4. Jack L. Goldsmith, "Will Donald Trump Destroy the Presidency?" *The Atlantic*, October 2017, https://www.theatlantic.com/magazine/archive /2017/10/will-donald-trump-destroy-the-presidency/537921/; Vanessa Sauter, "The Lawfare Podcast, Bonus Edition: Jack Goldsmith on the Norm-Defying Presidency," Lawfare (blog), October 3, 2017, https:// lawfareblog.com/lawfare-podcast-bonus-edition-jack-goldsmith-norm

-defying-presidency; Teresa Sullivan, "Sullivan's Message to UVA Community in Advance of Rally," August 4, 2017, https://news.virginia.edu /content/president-sullivan-condemns-demonstration-violence#sullivan _advance_letter.

5. Sullivan, "Sullivan's Message to UVA Community in Advance of Rally."

6. Dexter Thomas Tre'vell Anderson, "Jesse Williams Says Black Lives Matter—We Break Down Why His BET Speech Matters," *Los Angeles Times*, June 28, 2016, http://www.latimes.com/entertainment/music/la -et-st-jesse-williams-bet-annotated-20160627-snap-htmlstory.html.

7. "Ruby Bridges Biography," Biography.com, January 18, 2018, https:// www.biography.com/people/ruby-bridges-475426.

8. Robert Coles, *The Story of Ruby Bridges* (New York: Scholastic, 1995).

9. Jeanne Whalen, "The Children of the Opioid Crisis," *The Wall Street Journal*, December 15, 2016, https://www.wsj.com/articles/the-children -of-the-opioid-crisis-1481816178.

10. Helen Vendler, "Rita Dove: Identity Markers," in *The Given and the Made* (Cambridge, MA: Harvard University Press, 1995), 61.

11. Jason Felch, "No Gold Stars for Excellent L.A. Teaching," *Los Angeles Times*, August 29, 2010.

12. Amanda Ripley, "What Makes a Great Teacher?" *The Atlantic*, January–February 2010, https://www.theatlantic.com/magazine/archive/2010/01 /what-makes-a-great-teacher/307841/.

13. Jonathan Croall, *Neill of Summerhill: The Permanent Rebel* (New York: Routledge and Kegan Paul, 1983), 76, 102.

14. Will Brinson, "Here's How Nate Boyer Got Kaepernick to Go from Sitting to Kneeling," CBS Sports, September 27, 2016, https://www .cbssports.com/nfl/news/heres-how-nate-boyer-got-colin-kaepernick -to-go-from-sitting-to-kneeling/.

15. Jay-Z, "Most Kings," in *Decoded* (New York: Spiegel & Grau, 2011), 99; Joy Ann Reid (@joyannreid), Twitter, October 24, 2016, 5:30 p.m., https:// twitter.com/joyannreid/status/790712036397314048.

16. Sam Eifling (@SamEifling), Twitter, February 2, 2017, 9:46 a.m.

17. Brennan Williams, "Spike Lee Says Kaepernick Protest Similar to That of Ali," *Huffington Post*, September 1, 2016, https://www.huffingtonpost .com/entry/spike-lee-colin-kaepernicks-national-anthem-ali-protest _us_57c7315ce4b0a22de093c6ab.

18. Kyle Koster, "Colin Kaepernick: If I'm Killed, It Will Prove My Point and Speed Up Movement," The Big Lead (blog), September 21, 2016.

19. Actually,@eaton, Twitter, March 21, 2017, 4:19 p.m., https://twitter.com /eaton/status/844327588948533248.

20. "A Conversation Between Drew Faust and Leon Wieseltier," YouTube, published by Harvard Law School, April 16, 2015, https://www.youtube.com/watch?v=V4TXg69kfo8&t=3319s; Helen Vendler, *The Music of What Happens: Poems, Poets, Critics* (Cambridge, MA: Harvard University Press, 1988), 20.

21. Tim Pierce (@qwrrty), "Y'all should hear about my experience with BLM at the Boston Anti-Nazi Rally," Twitter, August 19, 2017, 1:02 p.m., https://twitter.com/qwrrty/status/898998545088299008.

5. STAMPED FROM THE BEGINNING

1. Sasha Frere-Jones, "On Top," *The New Yorker*, April 3, 2006, https://www.newyorker.com/magazine/2006/04/03/on-top.

2. Nikole Hannah-Jones, "Choosing a School for My Daughter in a Segregated City," *The New York Times Magazine*, June 9, 2016, https://www.nytimes.com/2016/06/12/magazine/choosing-a-school-for-my-daughter-in-a-segregated-city.html.

3. Henderson, email to Cinque Henderson, June 24, 2017.

4. "The Paradox of the Ghetto," *The Economist*, January 29, 2015, https://www.economist.com/news/britain/21641283-unnervingly-poor-children-seem-fare-better-poor-neighbourhoods-paradox-ghetto.

5. Corina Graif, "Delinquency and Gender Moderation in the Moving to Opportunity Intervention: The Role of Extended Neighborhoods," *Criminology*, August 18, 2015, http://onlinelibrary.wiley.com/doi/10.1111/1745-9125.12078/full; quote taken from Diana Goldstein, "Why It's Hard to Be a Poor Boy with Richer Neighbors," *The Marshall Project*, November 3, 2015.

6. Eleanor E. Maccoby, "The Two Sexes and Their Social Systems," in *The Nurture Assumption: Why Children Turn Out the Way They Do*, by Judith Harris (New York: Free Press, 1998), 229.

7. Ibid.

8. David Samuel, "The Rap on Rap," *The New Republic*, November 11, 1991.

9. Vanessa Friedman, "Jaden Smith for Louis Vuitton: The New Man in a Skirt," *The New York Times*, January 6, 2016, https://www.nytimes.com/2016/01/07/fashion/jaden-smith-for-louis-vuitton-the-new-man-in-a-skirt.html.

10. Damone Williams (@DamoneWilliams), Twitter, November 22, 2016, 2:18 p.m.

11. Ibram Kendi, *Stamped from the Beginning* (New York: Nation Books, 2016), 28, 34.

6. THE CHILD IS FATHER TO THE MAN

1. Ephesians 6:12.
2. Jean-Jacques Rousseau, *Emile*, Introduction by P. D. Jimack (London: J. M. Dent, 1974), 58.
3. Women Ruined My LIFE (@Mr_Alexius), Twitter, May 9, 2017, 7:13 a.m.; Trillhouse Van Houten (@Tre_Guevara), Twitter, May 9, 2017, 7:55 a.m.; Cammoji (@CoolGreyDreams), Twitter, May 9, 2017, 7:32 a.m.
4. Wallace Killmonger (@3xDopes), Twitter, May 9, 2017, 6:36 a.m.
5. Pilot Jones (@McKineb), Twitter, May 9, 2017, 6:27 a.m.
6. The Breakfast Club, "Remy Ma Takes over the Breakfast Club," YouTube video, 1:38:04, August 7, 2017.
7. Alfred A. Young, *Are Black Men Doomed?* (New York: Polity Press, 2018), 67.
8. Danielle Allen, *Cuz: The Life and Times of Michael A.* (New York: Liveright, 2017), 85.
9. Charles Siebert, "An Elephant Crackup?" *The New York Times Magazine*, October 8, 2006, http://www.nytimes.com/2006/10/08/magazine/08elephant.html.
10. Cinque Henderson, "Three Places Obama Could Teach," TheNewYorker .com, March 16, 2016, https://www.newyorker.com/news/news-desk/three-places-obama-could-teach.

7. LESS THAN ZERO TOLERANCE

1. California Attorney General's Office, Crime and Violence Prevention Center, *Gangs: A Statewide Directory of Programs, Intervention, Suppression* (Sacramento, 1994).
2. Retro Report, "Unraveling Zero Tolerance," TimesVideo, *The New York Times*, https://www.nytimes.com/video/us/100000004683057/unraveling-zero-tolerance.html.
3. "School-Based Enforcement Programs," report, Office of Juvenile Justice and Delinquency Prevention, https://www.ojjdp.gov/pubs/gun_violence/sect05-c.html.
4. Retro Report, "Unraveling Zero Tolerance."
5. Dirk Johnson, "Schools' New Watchword: Zero Tolerance," *The New York Times*, December 1, 1999, http://www.nytimes.com/1999/12/01/us/schools-new-watchword-zero-tolerance.html; Joe Clark clip, "Unraveling Zero Tolerance," at 2 minutes, 15 seconds, in *11th Hour: Joe Clark's Education*.

6. Johnson, "Schools' New Watchword."

7. Shay Bilchick, Office of Juvenile Justice and Delinquency Prevention, U.S. Department of Justice, *Promising Strategies to Reduce Gun Violence* (Washington, DC: U.S. Department of Justice, February 1999), 134, https://cops.usdoj.gov/html/cd_rom/solution_gang_crime/pubs/PromisingStrategiestoReduceGunViolence.pdf.

8. Jean-Jacques Rousseau, *Emile*, Introduction by P. D. Jimack (London: J. M. Dent, 1974), 10.

9. Chris Peak, "Suspending Students Isn't Effective. Here's What Schools Should Do Instead," *NationSwell*, March 27, 2015, http://nationswell.com/audubon-school-restorative-justice-reduces-suspensions/.

10. Teresa Watanabe and Howard Blume, "Why Some LAUSD Teachers Are Balking at a New Approach to Discipline Problems," *Los Angeles Times*, November 7, 2015, http://www.latimes.com/local/education/la-me-school-discipline-20151108-story.html.

11. Juan Perez Jr., "Teachers Complain About Revised CPS Discipline Policy," *Chicago Tribune*, February 25, 2015, http://www.chicagotribune.com/news/ct-cps-discipline-concerns-met-20150225-story.html.

12. Ibid.

13. "LAUSD Board Votes to End 'Willful Defiance' Suspension," CBS Los Angeles, May 15, 2013, http://losangeles.cbslocal.com/2013/05/15/lausd-board-votes-to-end-use-of-willful-defiance-suspensions/.

14. Watanabe and Blume, "Why Some LAUSD Teachers Are Balking at a New Approach to Discipline Problems."

15. Ibid. Emphasis is the author's.

8. FOLLOW THE MONEY

1. Milton Friedman, "The Role of Government in Education," in *Economics and the Public Interest*, edited by Robert Solo (New Jersey: Rutgers University Press, 1955), 3; Christopher and Sena Lubienski, *The Public School Advantage: Why Public Schools Outperform Private Ones* (Chicago: University of Chicago Press, 2013); Grace Hirshorn, "Investing in Writers," *The New Journal*, March 20, 2015, http://www.thenewjournalatyale.com/2015/03/investing-in-writers/.

2. Sarah Ruden, "How Harvard Helps Its Richest and Most Arrogant Students Get Ahead," op-ed, *The Washington Post*, September 19, 2017, https://www.washingtonpost.com/news/posteverything/wp/2017/09/19/how-harvard-helps-its-richest-and-most-arrogant-students-get-ahead/?utm_term=.2e08ba98e939.

3. Kurt Streeter, "South LA Student Finds a Different World at UC Berkeley," *Los Angeles Times*, August 16, 2013, http://www.latimes.com/local/la-me-cal-freshmen-20130816-m-story.html.

4. Davis Guggenheim, dir., *Waiting for Superman* (Santa Monica, CA: Electric Kinney Films, 2010).

5. Lyndsey Layton, "Charters Not Outperforming Nation's Traditional Public Schools, Report Says," *The Washington Post*, June 25, 2013, https://www.washingtonpost.com/local/education/charters-not-outperforming-nations-traditional-public-schools-report-says/2013/06/24/23f19bb8-dd0c-11e2-bd83-e99e43c336ed_story.html?utm_term=.3d52d3f4a7b3.

6. "Race and Ethnicity in Westlake, Los Angeles, California," *Statistical Atlas*, https://statisticalatlas.com/neighborhood/California/Los-Angeles/Westlake/Race-and-Ethnicity.

7. Times Editorial Board, "The Bias Inherent in Some Charter Schools' Admissions Process," op-ed, *Los Angeles Times*, August 10, 2016, http://www.latimes.com/opinion/editorials/la-ed-charter-application-20160808-snap-story.html.

8. "The Costs of Operating Small Schools in Oregon," Oregon Department of Education School Finance, Data and Analysis Office, October 25, 2002, http://www.oregon.gov/ode/reports-and-data/taskcomm/Documents/SFTF/2014.01.SFTFCostOfOperatingSmallSchoolsInOregon.pdf.

9. Centers for Disease Control, "Homicide, 1970–1979," February 7, 1986, http://www.cdc.gov/mmr/preview/mmwihtml/00000841.htm.

10. Spencer Rascoff, "Confirmed: Starbucks Knows the Next Hot Neighborhood Before Everyone Else Does," *Quartz*, January 28, 2015, https://qz.com/334269/what-starbucks-has-done-to-american-home-values/.

9. WHAT IT MEANS TO BE DISTRACTED

1. Walt Whitman, "A Noiseless Patient Spider," in *Leaves of Grass* (Philadelphia: David McKay, 1891).

2. Toni Morrison, *The Dancing Mind* (New York: Alfred A Knopf, 1996, 2003), 8–10.

3. Helen Vendler, "IA Richards at Harvard," *The Boston Review*, April 1, 1981, http://bostonreview.net/arts-culture/helen-vendler-i-richards-harvard.

4. J. D. Vance, *Hillbilly Elegy* (New York: HarperCollins, 2016), 138.

5. Don Ihde, *Listening and Voice* (Albany: State University of New York Press, 2007), 211, https://grrrr.org/data/edu/20110509-cascone/Idhe_listening_voice_phenomenologies.pdf.

6. Erik M. Altman and J. Gregory Trafton, "Momentary Interruptions Can Derail the Chain of Thought," *Journal of Experimental Psychology* 143, no. 1 (2014): 215–226, http://citeseerx.ist.psu.edu/viewdoc/download?doi=10.1.1.471.8248&rep=rep1&type=pdf.

7. Kurt Vonnegut, "Harrison Bergeron," https://archive.org/stream/HarrisonBergeron/Harrison%20Bergeron_djvu.txt.

8. Ibid.

10. FORGET IT, JAKE. IT'S CHINATOWN.

1. Cal Thomas, "Interview of Secretary of Education Betsy DeVos," *Townhall*, February 16, 2015, https://townhall.com/columnists/calthomas/2017/02/16/interview-of-secretary-of-education-betsy-devos-n2286164.

2. Jefferson Academy (@JATrojans), Twitter, February 17, 2017, 5:30 p.m.

3. Dani McClain, "To Improve School Discipline, Change *Teacher* Behavior," *Slate*, January 22, 2015, http://www.slate.com/blogs/schooled/2015/01/22/school_discipline_bay_area_schools_cut_down_on_suspensions_by_targeting.html.

INDEX

SAT tutoring, 165–166
Scarlet Letter, The (Hawthorne),
    172–173
school choice, 145–168, 219. *See also*
    charter schools
school vouchers, 5, 148–149
Second Persian Gulf War, 44
segregated schools, 23, 64–65, 81–82
self-control, 54–55, 65–67, 69–70, 74,
    76, 139, 146, 178. *See also*
    impulse control
self-creation, 177
self-hating, 5
self-image, 37, 103, 104
self-worth, 91, 98, 101, 114
separation as consequence of
    behavior, 50–53
September 11, 2001, 44, 47
sexism, 86, 89, 139
sexuality, 86–87
    homophobia, 86, 139
    puberty, 37–38, 110, 113
    sexualization of black men,
        103–104
Shakespeare, William, 68, 104
Shakur, Tupac, 24
Shanté, Roxanne, 87
Sharpton, Al, 89
Simpson, O. J., 91n
skin-color fetish, 90–94, 97–105, 107,
    184
small schools, 158–159, 162, 179
Smith, Jada Pinkett, 24
Smith, Jaden, 100
social promotion, 154
socialization, 49, 102, 162, 167, 219
socioeconomics, 18–19
    charter schools and, 154–157
    stringency and, 50–51
Socrates, 8
Sopranos, The (television drama),
    33–34
Southern Christian Leadership
    Conference, 75
"Special Story of Ms. Thompson,
    The," 193–195
Spelman College, 89–90
Spiegel, Elizabeth, 52–53
Stamped from the Beginning (Kendi),
    103
Starbucks, 164–165
stringency (consequences for actions)

elimination of, 47, 49–50, 53, 68,
    78–79, 132, 139–143, 152, 180,
    186
    necessity of, 45, 53–55, 66–69
    parenting and, 138, 142
    purpose of, 54–55, 74
    racial disparities and, 50, 79
    separation as, 50–53
    socioeconomic disparities and,
        50–51
    soft power and, 49
    sweetness and soft power combined
        with, 10, 43, 49, 74, 115, 162, 220
    thriving schools and, 66–69
    See also detention; expulsion;
        reform schools; suspension
substitute teaching, 4–7
    automated system for, 12n
    every day as first day of school, 12
    student impulse control and, 33
    "Super Sub," 210–211
*Summerhill: A Radical Approach to
    Child Rearing* (Neill), 16
Summerhill Academy, 15–17, 65–67
Supreme Court
    Brown v. Board of Education, 64
    protestors at, 51, 53
suspension
    alternative schools and, 143, 220
    economic impact of, 158, 166
    detentions and, 49, 79, 139
    elimination of, 47, 49–50, 53, 68,
        78, 132, 139–143, 152, 180, 186
    purpose of, 45, 54
    racial disparity and, 50, 79
    reinstating, 220
    restorative justice and, 49, 140
    zero tolerance policies and,
        135–136
    See also stringency
swearing. *See* cursing
Syria, 139

Tan, Zenaida, 67–68
tax reform, 122
Taylor, William, 68–69
Teach for America (TFA), 128–129,
    131n, 146, 164–165
teachers
    assaults on, 4, 46, 48, 67, 141, 193
    black male teachers, 119, 220
    cursing at, 1–3, 15, 34–35, 43, 46,